HIDDEN CORNERS OF LONDON 2026

Discover London's Hidden Architecture, Forgotten Streets, and Local Secrets

By:
Selene draxwell

Copyright © 2025 Selene draxwell

No part of this publication may be reproduced, distributed, or transmitted in any form or by any means, including photocopying, recording, or other electronic or mechanical methods, without the prior written permission of the publisher, except in the case of brief quotations embodied in critical reviews and certain other non-commercial uses permitted by copyright law.

Table of Content

MAP Of London 7

INTRODUCTION 9

Chapter 1 15

Before You Wander: Preparing for the Hidden London Experience 15
    1. What Makes London's Hidden Corners So Special 16
    2. How to Plan Beyond the Tourist Map 16
    3. Must-Have Documents and Travel Apps 17
    4. Packing for Exploration: From Cobblestone Streets to Canal Paths 18
    5. Apps, Maps & Tools for Offbeat Adventures 19
    6. *Local Secret:* Why Locals Keep Certain Places Quiet 20

Chapter 2 22

Finding Your Way: Getting In and Around Like a Local 22
    1. Arriving in London: Airports, Trains, and the Secret Shortcuts .. 23
    2. The Underground and Overground: Stops with Hidden Stories . 24
    3. Bus Routes to Unexpected Views 25
    4. Exploring by Foot and Bicycle: Quiet Routes and Riverside Paths 25
    5. *Insider Tip:* Where Londoners Escape During Rush Hour 26

Chapter 3 28

Where to Stay Off the Beaten Path 28
    1. Character-Filled Neighborhoods: From Hampstead Lanes to Peckham Streets 29
    2. Boutique Guesthouses and Converted Warehouses 30
    3. Sleep Among History: Unusual Stays in Former Schools, Churches, and Pubs 31
    4. Choosing the Right Area for Hidden Discoveries 31
    5. *Mistake to Avoid:* Staying Too Central and Missing the Real London 32

Chapter 4 34

London's Story Beneath the Surface 34
1. Layers of Time: The City's Forgotten Eras and Overlooked Heroes 34
2. Underground History: Abandoned Tube Stations and Hidden Tunnels 35
3. Secret Architecture: Mews, Courtyards, and Lost Villages 36
4. The City Within a City: The Secrets of the Square Mile 37

Chapter 5 40

Food with a Local Twist: Eating Beyond the Usual 40
1. Hidden Markets and Tiny Cafés That Locals Love 40
2. Family-Run Restaurants and Pop-Ups in Unexpected Places..... 41
3. Historic Pubs, Secret Bars, and Rooftop Hideaways 42
4. The London You Can Taste: Street Food with a Story 43
5. *Insider Tip:* Where Chefs Eat on Their Day Off 44

Chapter 6 45

Neighborhood Secrets: The Soul of the Hidden City...45
1. North London: Secret Gardens of Hampstead & Railway Bridges of Camden 45
2. East London: Street Art Alleys and Old Warehouses Turned Galleries 46
3. South London: Dulwich Lanes, Forest Hill Cafés & Crystal Palace Ruins 47
4. West London: Notting Hill's Quiet Streets and Hammersmith's Riverside Corners 49

Chapter 7 51

Time Travel — Hidden Historic and Cultural Sites of London 51
1. Lesser-Known Churches, Crypts, and Cemeteries 51
2. Small Museums with Big Stories 52
3. Forgotten Palaces and Gardens of the Aristocracy...................... 53
4. Theatres, Record Shops, and Studios That Shaped London's Art Scene 53
5. Mistake to Avoid: Visiting the Big Landmarks First 54

Chapter 8 56
Seasons in the Shadows: When to Explore 56
1. London in Spring: Secret Gardens and Blossom Walks 56
2. Summer Escapes: Quiet Parks and Hidden Rooftops 57
3. Autumn Discoveries: Leafy Lanes and Candlelit Pubs 58
4. Winter Magic: Hidden Markets and Cozy Corners 59
5. Packing Note: What to Wear When Exploring Hidden Streets ... 60

Chapter 9 62
Itineraries for Every Curious Traveler 62
1. One Day: Quick Hidden Highlights 62
2. Three Days: Explore the City's Overlooked Gems 63
3. A Week or More: Deep Dive into Local Life 63
4. Themed Trails: Secret Gardens, Forgotten Stations, Literary Corners 64
5. Insider Tip: Mixing Popular and Hidden Spots for Balance 65

Chapter 10 66
Practical Wisdom for Urban Explorers 66
1. Staying Safe While Going Off the Beaten Path 66
2. Budgeting Smartly for Unique Experiences 67
3. Navigating Language, Etiquette, and Humor 68
4. Apps, Emergency Numbers, and Local Contacts 69
5. Mistake to Avoid: Ignoring Local Advice 69

Chapter 11 71
Meeting the Real Londoners 71
1. How to Strike Up Conversation in Local Pubs and Markets 71
2. Volunteering and Community Events for Visitors 72
3. Creative Workshops and Neighborhood Classes 73
4. Local Secret: The Londoners Who Know the City's Soul 73

Chapter 12 75
Capturing the Hidden Side 75
1. Photographing the City Without Crowds 75
2. Journaling Your Discoveries 76
3. Social Media Without Spoiling the Secrets 77

4. Reflection: How Hidden Corners Change the Way You See London 78

Chapter 13 .... *80*

Beyond Goodbye — Keep the Spirit of Discovery Alive **80**

1. Returning for More: Hidden Corners You Missed This Time 80
2. Similar European Cities with the Same Quiet Charm 81
3. Staying in Touch with Locals and Fellow Travelers 82
4. Sustainable Exploration: Respecting the Spaces You Find 82

Conclusion *84*

MAP OF LONDON

Access the map by scanning the QR code

INTRODUCTION

Have you ever wondered how many stories hide behind closed doors? How many lives have unfolded in streets you've never noticed, or in buildings you've walked past without a second glance? London is filled with such moments — tiny fragments of time tucked between the familiar and the forgotten. The city you think you know is only one version of it. There are others, quieter ones, waiting behind side streets, in unmarked courtyards, and down staircases that lead to places most visitors never find.

What if the real spirit of a city isn't found in its landmarks, but in the spaces between them? The quiet pub where locals gather after work, the bench beneath an old tree in a park that doesn't appear on any guide, the corner shop where conversation flows more freely than the till rings. London is full of these fragments — places that ask you to slow down, to notice the details, to listen rather than look. The city doesn't shout about them; it never has. You simply have to wander with the right kind of curiosity.

It's easy to think of London as loud, hurried, and always in motion. The Underground roars beneath your feet, the buses surge past, and every crossing light feels like a countdown. Yet beneath that rush lies another rhythm. You find it in a quiet morning along the Regent's Canal, when mist softens the edges of moored boats. You hear it in the sound of footsteps echoing under railway arches near Southwark. You feel it in the stillness of a hidden garden behind tall brick walls in Bloomsbury. If you pause long enough, the noise fades, and a different kind of London begins to reveal itself — slower, more personal, and astonishingly alive.

Have you ever noticed how some of the most memorable moments in travel happen by accident? You set out to visit a museum and end up finding a secondhand bookshop that changes your afternoon. You miss a train and discover a tiny café that serves the best coffee you've ever tasted. You follow a street because of the way the sunlight hits the pavement, and suddenly you're somewhere entirely unexpected. That's the beauty of exploring beyond the obvious — the discoveries that can't be planned, only found. London rewards that kind of wandering spirit more than most places.

Every corner here has something to say. An old doorway might hold a bullet mark from the Blitz. A narrow alley in the East End might trace a line that hasn't changed since medieval times. Even the graffiti on a brick wall might tell a story about protest, love, or local pride. The city speaks in textures — cobblestones, soot-stained stone, wrought iron, and glass. It's a place that wears its history openly, yet keeps its best secrets hidden in plain sight.

What makes this city so endlessly fascinating is its ability to reinvent itself without ever letting go of the past. The same street can hold a centuries-old pub and a minimalist art gallery, and somehow, both feel completely at home. A Georgian terrace might hide a jazz club in its basement. A Victorian warehouse could now house a community theatre. London never erases; it layers. And in those layers, you find its hidden corners — traces of everything that came before, mingling with what is happening right now.

If you listen to Londoners, they'll tell you that everyone has their own version of the city. For some, it's the skyline seen from Waterloo Bridge at dusk. For others, it's the chatter of a market on a Saturday morning, the smell of rain on hot pavement, or the sudden quiet of an empty street after midnight. But ask a lifelong resident, and you'll often hear about a small place that means more than any landmark — a tiny bakery that's been there forever, a park bench with a view only they know, a passageway that connects two familiar streets in a way tourists rarely notice. These are the places that turn the city from a destination into a companion.

You can spend a lifetime here and still not see everything. That's the charm and the challenge of London. It isn't a city that reveals itself easily. It asks for patience, for openness, for the willingness to wander without a checklist. Sometimes, the best discoveries happen when you stop trying to find them. The cobbled lane behind a church in Clerkenwell, the garden square in Fitzrovia that feels like a secret shared among residents, the café in Hackney that still uses mismatched furniture and serves coffee that tastes like it's been made with care rather than precision — these are the stories that never make it into glossy brochures, yet they're the ones you'll remember most vividly.

Have you ever noticed how different cities feel depending on how you move through them? In London, walking is everything. The Underground will take you anywhere, but your feet will take you further. Some of the best experiences happen between stations — that short stretch from Holborn to Covent Garden, the stroll from Borough Market to the river, the gentle climb up to Primrose Hill. Along the way, you'll notice things others miss: small plaques that mark forgotten lives, fading shop signs from another era, and window boxes overflowing with flowers where you least expect them. Walking slows you down enough to let the city speak.

The hidden corners aren't just physical spaces — they're also found in the way Londoners live. You see it in community markets that pop up under railway bridges, in supper clubs hosted in strangers' homes, in small theatres that run on volunteers and passion rather than fame. You hear it in the street musicians at Covent Garden, in the laughter spilling from late-night kebab shops, in the conversations that drift across tables in old pubs. It's the feeling that this enormous city, despite its size, is built from small, human moments.

There's also the matter of perspective. Most visitors look up at London — at its skyline, its monuments, its architecture. But some of its most interesting stories lie below or behind. Old tunnels under Aldwych Station tell of forgotten train lines. A hidden Roman temple sits beneath a modern office building. A walled garden in Chelsea remains almost unchanged since the seventeenth century. Even in the busiest areas, there's always a doorway, an alley, or a courtyard that leads to something unexpected. The city rewards curiosity, and it always has.

Do you remember the last time a place surprised you? Not with grandeur, but with simplicity — the sudden sight of flowers growing through cracked pavement, the way light hits an old window at dusk, the discovery of a mural tucked behind a car park. London offers those moments constantly, if you're willing to notice them. They're not staged, not curated, and not designed to impress. They're what happens when life and history quietly coexist.

Sometimes, the stories behind these places are what make them special. A narrow passageway might once have been used by servants delivering bread to grand houses. A small church might have sheltered residents during air raids. A quiet mews might have been home to stable boys who later became artists, writers, or simply names lost to time. When you explore beyond the main streets, you start to sense these invisible histories pressing up against the present. It's a feeling both humbling and thrilling —

that you're walking through layers of lives, each one leaving a trace behind.

Of course, every discovery comes with a sense of connection. The more you wander, the more you start to see patterns — how locals greet one another in the same corner café, how market traders remember returning customers, how a street musician always plays the same tune at the same time each day. It's in those observations that you begin to understand London not as a maze to navigate, but as a living, breathing collection of neighborhoods. Each one has its own rhythm, shaped by the people who pass through it and those who never leave.

What makes these places "hidden" isn't secrecy — it's familiarity. Locals walk these streets daily, unaware they're special, while visitors rush past searching for something more recognizable. But when you slow down and look with fresh eyes, even the ordinary turns extraordinary. The mural you pass each day changes with the weather. The same bench offers a different view depending on the season. The sound of the city shifts with the hour. That's what makes exploration so endlessly rewarding here — no two moments are ever the same.

There's a particular joy in feeling lost and comfortable at the same time. In London, that happens often. One moment you're navigating a quiet residential street, and the next you stumble upon a pub that feels like it's been waiting just for you. The city has a way of balancing familiarity and surprise, of offering both refuge and adventure. It invites you to wander without purpose, to follow instinct rather than itinerary. That's when it feels most alive.

You might begin your exploration chasing the hidden corners others have mentioned, but soon you'll start to find your own. Maybe it's a small courtyard near St. Paul's where the bells echo differently in the morning air. Maybe it's a bakery in Notting Hill that smells of cardamom and nostalgia. Or maybe it's simply a view from a bridge at twilight, when the river reflects both the lights of the present and the shadows of the past. These discoveries are personal. No guide or map can give them to you; they happen because you let the city surprise you.

As you wander, you'll notice how every part of London holds its own kind of silence. Even in the busiest markets or busiest streets, there's always a corner where time seems to pause — a moment between footsteps, a gap between conversations. These are the spaces where you begin to feel not like a visitor, but like a participant in the story unfolding around you. You start to see how the city carries its memories gently, never erasing but always renewing.

Perhaps that's why so many people fall for this place — not because of what it shows, but because of what it hides. The greatest reward of exploring these lesser-known corners isn't simply discovering something beautiful; it's realizing that beauty has always been there, waiting for someone to notice. The thrill isn't in ticking off locations but in forming small, lasting connections — with people, with places, and with moments that feel entirely your own.

When you leave, you'll find that London lingers. The sounds, the scents, the small discoveries — they stay with you longer than any photograph can. You might forget a museum, but you'll remember a conversation with a shopkeeper who shared a story about the street you were standing on. You might forget the price of a ticket, but not the feeling of finding a hidden garden after the rain. That's the kind of travel that changes how you see a city — and how you see yourself in it.

So when you set out to explore, don't rush. Don't try to see everything. Walk, pause, listen, and let the city unfold naturally. Because here, discovery isn't a checklist — it's a state of mind. And once you've seen London this way, you'll never see it the same again.

Chapter 1

Before You Wander: Preparing for the Hidden London Experience

There's a London that most visitors never see. It's not the London of postcards and souvenir shops, but the one tucked behind narrow alleys, hidden beneath train arches, and whispered about in quiet corners of cafés. It's a city that reveals itself only to those who slow down, look closer, and wander without a plan. But before you begin exploring those lesser-known corners, there are a few things you should know. Preparation can turn a good trip into an unforgettable one — and in a city as full of surprises as London, being prepared means you'll spot the moments others miss.

1. What Makes London's Hidden Corners So Special

What makes some places so easily missed? Maybe it's because they don't advertise themselves. The beauty of London's hidden corners lies in their subtlety — the way they exist quietly between the noise of double-decker buses and the buzz of Oxford Street. These are the places that locals stumble upon on a rainy afternoon, the ones that never make it to glossy travel brochures.

Take Neal's Yard, for example. Just off the busy Covent Garden streets, you'll find a burst of color — small cafés, independent shops, and bright murals tucked inside a courtyard so well-hidden that you could walk past it a dozen times and never know. Or think about Postman's Park, where small plaques quietly tell stories of everyday heroes who gave their lives to save others. These spots remind you that London's charm doesn't always shout; sometimes it whispers.

So why do these places matter? Because they reveal something real — a side of the city shaped by people rather than landmarks. Every alleyway and market stall has a story, every pub corner has a memory. Exploring these spaces lets you feel the heartbeat of local life, the rhythm that tourists often miss when they rush from one famous attraction to the next. The reward isn't just what you see, but how you see it.

And here's the thing: discovering hidden corners changes the way you experience the whole city. It encourages curiosity, patience, and a sense of adventure that guidebooks alone can't give you. It turns a trip into a treasure hunt — and the clues are everywhere if you're paying attention.

2. How to Plan Beyond the Tourist Map

Have you ever found yourself staring at a tourist map that highlights all the same spots — the Tower, the Eye, the Bridge —

and thought, "There must be more"? There is. But to find it, you have to plan differently. Instead of asking, "What should I see?" try asking, "What do locals enjoy when no one's watching?"

Planning beyond the tourist map starts with curiosity. Forget about checking off attractions and focus instead on experiences. For instance, swap Buckingham Palace for the backstreets of Bermondsey, where you'll find hidden gin distilleries and food markets inside old railway arches. Or skip Leicester Square and spend an evening in a small music bar in Camden, where unsigned bands play to loyal crowds.

A simple trick is to plan your days around themes instead of places. You could dedicate one afternoon to "hidden green spaces," exploring spots like the Kyoto Garden in Holland Park or Phoenix Garden in Soho. Another day could be "secret histories," visiting places like the Roman Temple of Mithras buried beneath Bloomberg's offices, or the Churchill War Rooms where the decisions that shaped modern history were made.

Local blogs, community boards, and neighborhood Facebook groups can be more useful than traditional travel sites. They're where residents share recent pop-ups, independent markets, and festivals that rarely make it into mainstream travel articles. And remember: spontaneity is part of the fun. Leave space in your plan for detours — because the best finds often come when you take a wrong turn.

3. Must-Have Documents and Travel Apps

Nothing ruins an adventure faster than paperwork problems or getting lost without help. Before you wander into London's hidden corners, make sure you've got your essentials sorted.

For most visitors, a valid passport and, if needed, a visa are your top priorities. Check your visa requirements before you travel — not at the airport queue. It's also smart to make digital copies of your documents (passport, ID, travel insurance, and bookings) and store them in a secure cloud folder or app. Losing your phone or wallet can be stressful, but digital backups make recovery much easier.

Now, let's talk about tools that make life simpler. **Citymapper** is your best friend for navigating London's complex transport network — it shows you the fastest routes by tube, bus, or even bicycle. **Google Maps** is great for directions, but don't overlook **Hidden London** or **Spotted by Locals** — apps designed to uncover places that locals love but tourists overlook.

If you like exploring at your own pace, **VoiceMap** offers self-guided walking tours narrated by locals. For keeping travel documents organized, **TripIt** and **Notion Travel Planner** can keep your itineraries tidy. And since cashless payments are everywhere, apps like **Revolut** or **Wise** can help you manage your money without bank fees.

The key is balance: technology should guide you, not control you. A paper map might seem old-fashioned, but in London's winding streets — where GPS signals sometimes fail — it can be a lifesaver. And there's something satisfying about tracing your path with a pen and realizing how far your feet have taken you.

4. Packing for Exploration: From Cobblestone Streets to Canal Paths

What do you really need to bring when your plan is to wander? Packing for hidden corners means thinking less about style and more about practicality. You'll be walking a lot — through uneven cobblestones, narrow staircases, canal paths, and hidden gardens — so comfortable shoes are essential. Choose waterproof ones if you can; London's weather has a mind of its own.

Layering is key. The city can shift from sunny to chilly in minutes, especially near the Thames. A light rain jacket or compact umbrella should always have a place in your bag. Opt for a backpack instead of a suitcase when exploring — one that fits a water bottle, a notebook, and maybe a small snack. You'll thank yourself when you're wandering through markets or hopping on a bus.

When it comes to clothing, blend in with locals: simple, practical, and weather-ready. Flashy "tourist" outfits attract attention in the wrong way. Keep valuables like jewelry or expensive cameras subtle and secure. For photography, a smartphone often does the job beautifully — and it's easier to handle when moving through busy areas.

If you plan to explore at night, pack a small flashlight or use your phone's torch. Some of the city's most charming lanes are dimly lit, adding to the mystery but making it easy to trip over uneven ground. A reusable shopping bag is another must-have — many of the city's independent shops and markets don't hand out free plastic ones anymore.

Think of packing as preparation for discovery. The lighter you pack, the more freedom you'll have to wander wherever curiosity leads. After all, it's hard to enjoy a hidden canal path if your shoulders ache from carrying too much.

5. Apps, Maps & Tools for Offbeat Adventures

London's hidden corners might not be marked with bold signs, but that doesn't mean they're impossible to find. The right digital companions can turn your phone into a personal guide without spoiling the adventure.

Start with **Google Maps**' satellite view. Zoom in on unfamiliar neighborhoods, and you'll often spot courtyards, alleyways, and gardens that aren't labeled. Tap on businesses or landmarks with few reviews — those often lead to genuine hidden gems. **Atlas Obscura** is another gem itself, showcasing offbeat spots like abandoned theaters, secret gardens, and underground bars.

If you're into walking routes, **Komoot** and **AllTrails** aren't just for hikers — they feature urban walks too, including riverside paths and old railway trails. Pair those with **Time Out London** or **Secret London** for updated lists of pop-up events and quirky cafés.

For social explorers, **Meetup** and **Eventbrite** are excellent for finding small local gatherings — photography walks, poetry nights, vintage market meetups. These tools help you experience the city the way locals do: through community, not crowds.

Still, remember that no app can replace the joy of discovery. Sometimes, the best "tool" is your instinct — following an interesting smell from a bakery, a distant melody from a busker, or the laughter echoing down a side street. Let technology assist, not lead.

6. *Local Secret:* Why Locals Keep Certain Places Quiet

Ever wondered why Londoners sometimes hesitate to share their favorite spots? It's not selfishness — it's preservation. Hidden corners survive because they stay small, personal, and uncommercialized. Once too many people know about them, the magic changes.

Think about a quiet riverside café where artists sketch in peace. Or an old bookshop that feels frozen in time. These places rely on a steady rhythm of regulars, not tourist floods. Locals protect them the way you'd protect a secret recipe — by sharing it only with people who will appreciate it.

If you're lucky enough to find one of these special corners, treat it gently. Buy something small from the shop, greet the owner, leave a kind review if appropriate — but resist tagging every spot on social media. Sometimes the most memorable experiences are the ones you keep to yourself.

Respecting local spaces also means being mindful. Keep noise low, support small businesses, and avoid blocking narrow walkways with big groups or tripods. These places thrive because of respect — and by showing it, you become part of what keeps them alive.

Exploring hidden London isn't about covering the most ground; it's about seeing what most overlook. Preparation — both practical and mental — is what allows you to truly experience the city beneath the surface. When you're ready, take that first step off the main road and into a quiet lane. Listen to the echoes of the past, the hum of daily life, the stories hidden in the bricks. That's where the real adventure begins.

Chapter 2

Finding Your Way: Getting In and Around Like a Local

Getting around London can feel like both a challenge and an adventure. The city stretches far and wide, with layers of history running under its streets and surprises waiting around every corner. But here's the good news: once you learn how London moves, you'll find it's one of the easiest cities to navigate. Every station, street, and shortcut tells its own story. The trick is knowing where to look—and how to move like a local.

Most first-time visitors focus on big attractions and familiar transport lines, but the real experience begins when you look beyond the obvious. This chapter helps you do just that—whether you're stepping off a plane at Heathrow, catching a train into Paddington, or gliding along the Thames on a river bus. It's about more than routes and maps—it's about rhythm and awareness.

You'll discover hidden paths, local shortcuts, and a few tricks that even some Londoners haven't noticed.

1. Arriving in London: Airports, Trains, and the Secret Shortcuts

Landing in London can be exciting but also a little overwhelming. With six major airports and several big train stations, it's easy to feel lost before your adventure even begins. But don't worry—London's transport network is built to connect everything.

The main airports—Heathrow, Gatwick, Stansted, Luton, London City, and Southend—each have their own personality. Heathrow is the busiest and feels like a small city of its own. If you're flying into Heathrow, the Heathrow Express is the fastest way into central London, taking you straight to Paddington Station in about 15 minutes. But here's something locals know: the cheaper option is the Elizabeth Line. It takes a little longer but costs less, and it's just as comfortable.

Arriving at Gatwick? The Gatwick Express runs to Victoria Station, but regular Southern trains take the same route for less money. A little patience saves a lot of pounds. If you land at Stansted or Luton, you'll arrive in north London—both connect to the city by train within an hour. London City Airport, though smaller, is a favorite for those staying in central areas; the Docklands Light Railway (DLR) connects directly to key Tube stations.

Now, about those "secret shortcuts." Paddington, King's Cross, and Victoria are more than transport hubs—they're gateways to hidden London. From Paddington, stroll along the Regent's Canal toward Little Venice. It's peaceful, lined with houseboats and cafés, and feels miles away from the busy streets above. From King's Cross, instead of rushing to the Underground, take a short walk to Coal Drops Yard—a redeveloped area full of quiet corners, art spaces, and great food. These moments of calm are what make travel in London special—you just need to know they're there.

2. The Underground and Overground: Stops with Hidden Stories

Every visitor learns about the Tube. It's fast, efficient, and iconic. But here's the thing: the Underground isn't just transport—it's history. Each station hides stories from the past. Did you know that Aldwych Station was used as a bomb shelter during World War II? Or that the tiles at Covent Garden still show signs of early 1900s design? Even the map itself is legendary—simple, colorful, and unchanged since 1933.

The Overground, often overlooked by tourists, is a hidden gem. It runs above ground, linking neighborhoods that most visitors never see—places like Hackney, Highbury, and Peckham. These areas are full of creativity, local markets, and lesser-known cafés. Want a real London experience? Hop on the Overground and ride between Shoreditch High Street and Crystal Palace. You'll see street art, historic stations, and a side of London that doesn't appear in travel brochures.

For a quiet moment underground, explore stations like St. James's Park or Great Portland Street. They're some of the oldest on the network and often much calmer than their busy neighbors. And here's a local secret: if you stand at the front of the Northern Line train going northbound from London Bridge, you can catch a brief glimpse of the old abandoned City Road station—a ghost of London's transport past.

So yes, the Underground can be crowded, but it's also alive with stories. Locals often say you haven't truly met London until you've stood shoulder to shoulder on a Tube train during rush hour. But don't worry—you'll learn when to ride, when to walk, and when to look for that little-known shortcut that saves both time and sanity.

3. Bus Routes to Unexpected Views

London's red buses aren't just a symbol—they're one of the best ways to see the city. Tour buses may promise "panoramic views," but locals know the regular routes offer the same sights for a fraction of the cost. Take the number 11 from Liverpool Street to Chelsea—it passes landmarks like St. Paul's Cathedral, Trafalgar Square, and Westminster Abbey. The number 24 runs past Camden, Regent's Park, and the West End. And the 15 offers a nostalgic ride through old London streets in vintage-style buses.

But there's more to buses than sightseeing. They connect neighborhoods that the Tube skips. From Hampstead Heath to Greenwich, you can explore local life without ever stepping underground. Sitting upstairs, near the front, gives you a view that feels cinematic—especially at night when the city glows.

Hidden corners? Try the number 9, which glides through Kensington and along Piccadilly—two areas rich with quiet architecture and elegant streets. Or ride the 87 from Aldwych to Wandsworth; it follows the Thames for part of the way, giving glimpses of bridges and riverside walkways that most tourists miss.

For those who prefer peace and patience, buses reveal how London really breathes—slowly, through everyday life. You'll see people reading, chatting, gazing out windows, and you'll start to notice details you'd never spot underground.

4. Exploring by Foot and Bicycle: Quiet Routes and Riverside Paths

Some of London's best discoveries can't be reached by train or bus. They're hidden behind narrow lanes, tucked between parks, or sitting quietly beside the water. Walking or cycling opens those doors.

One of the city's best-kept secrets is the Regent's Canal walk, stretching from Little Venice to Limehouse. Along the way, you'll pass through Camden Lock's buzzing market, Regent's Park's tranquil edges, and hidden cafes beneath bridges. The entire route feels like a story told in stages—each turn revealing a different mood.

If you're near the Thames, follow the South Bank trail from Westminster Bridge to Tower Bridge. The path winds past street performers, book stalls, and quiet benches perfect for watching the city flow by. Want something even calmer? Cross to the north side and explore the narrow lanes of Wapping or Rotherhithe. These areas once thrived with sailors and traders; now they offer quiet pubs, cobbled streets, and riverside paths where you can walk for miles without crowds.

Cycling is another joy—especially using the city's bike-sharing system. Locals often use these bikes for short, scenic rides. Try pedaling through Hyde Park early in the morning or along the quiet back streets of Marylebone. On Sundays, many streets in central London are calmer, making it the perfect time to explore by pedal.

Here's something few visitors realize: London is full of "green corridors"—linked parks and pathways that let you move across large parts of the city without much traffic. From Hampstead Heath to Primrose Hill to Regent's Park, you can walk for hours through nature while still being in one of the biggest cities on Earth.

5. *Insider Tip:* Where Londoners Escape During Rush Hour

Ask any Londoner about rush hour, and you'll get a sigh and a smile. Trains packed, buses full, streets crowded—it's the daily rhythm of city life. But locals have their ways of escaping it.

If you find yourself in central London between 5 and 7 p.m., don't fight the crowd. Instead, do what the locals do—pause and enjoy the in-between time. Find a café near a quiet square, grab a seat, and let the chaos pass. Covent Garden has tiny lanes just behind the main piazza where you can breathe again. In Soho, St. Anne's Churchyard offers benches shaded by trees and far from the noise.

For something more scenic, head to the river. The Thames Path between Blackfriars and London Bridge is usually peaceful at dusk. Watch the boats glide past and the city lights flicker on—it's one of those simple, grounding moments that remind you why London feels timeless.

And if you must travel, take the long way. Walking from Bank to St. Paul's or from Waterloo to the Strand might seem longer, but it's often faster than squeezing into a packed Tube. Plus, you'll stumble upon bookshops, food stalls, and corners of history along the way.

Moving through London doesn't have to be stressful or confusing. It can be one of the most rewarding parts of your journey. The city's transport system isn't just about getting from point A to point B—it's a story, a rhythm, a pulse that ties the old and new together. Whether you're stepping off a plane, swiping your Oyster card, or strolling along the canal, every path has something to teach you.

Ask yourself: where might the next turn lead? Could that small alley open to a hidden garden? Could that side street reveal a mural you'll never forget? In London, the answers are always waiting just around the corner.

CHAPTeR 3

WHERE TO STAY OFF THE BEATEN PATH

Sometimes, finding a place to stay in London feels like a puzzle. You search, scroll, and compare — yet many travelers still end up in the same predictable areas: the heart of the city, close to major landmarks, surrounded by chain hotels and tourist crowds. But what if the real London — the one that locals love and that travelers rarely see — waits just a few streets further out? Choosing where to stay isn't only about convenience; it shapes the way you experience the city. Let's explore how to find accommodation that makes you feel part of London's quieter, richer, more authentic side.

1. Character-Filled Neighborhoods: From Hampstead Lanes to Peckham Streets

Every city has its quieter corners, and London hides some of its best behind leafy streets and old shopfronts. Staying in these neighborhoods allows you to wake up to the rhythm of local life instead of the hum of tourist buses. Have you ever wondered what it's like to start your day with the sound of a milk float, a neighbor's radio, or the smell of freshly baked bread from a family-run bakery? That's what these areas offer — a slower, truer version of the city.

Take **Hampstead**, for instance. Its cobbled lanes, old cottages, and bookshops make it feel like a small village within a metropolis. You can walk through Hampstead Heath at sunrise, climb Parliament Hill for one of the best skyline views, and end your day in a candle-lit pub that hasn't changed much in a century.

Then there's **Peckham**, once overlooked, now buzzing with creativity but still rough-edged in the best way. Converted factories house art studios and rooftop bars, while street food stalls fill the air with Caribbean spices and Nigerian suya smoke. The energy feels real — not polished for visitors but honest and expressive.

If you prefer something more tranquil, **Stoke Newington** might be your match. Known for its independent spirit, it's full of cozy cafés, vintage shops, and green spaces like Clissold Park. You'll see parents pushing prams, friends chatting outside delis, and musicians carrying guitars — an everyday charm that never feels staged.

Staying in these neighborhoods means trading hotel uniformity for a sense of place. It's not only about where you sleep but how the streets outside your door make you feel — curious, inspired, and comfortable enough to wander without a map.

2. Boutique Guesthouses and Converted Warehouses

If you've grown tired of hotel chains that look identical in every city, London's smaller stays will feel like a revelation. Boutique guesthouses and converted buildings give you something rare — personality. These are places where the owners greet you by name, where breakfast might include homemade marmalade, and where every corner tells a story.

In **Notting Hill**, you'll find pastel-colored guesthouses with just a handful of rooms, often run by families who've lived there for generations. Each one feels like stepping into a carefully kept secret. A bookshelf filled with novels instead of tourist leaflets, antique furniture that creaks slightly, or framed photos of old London — details that turn a simple room into an experience.

Meanwhile, across the river in **Bermondsey**, old warehouses have found new life. Once part of London's industrial backbone, they now house stylish lofts and design-led hotels with exposed brick walls and art installations. Imagine waking up surrounded by history yet surrounded by modern comfort — a blend that defines London's constant reinvention.

Even smaller towns within the city, like **Walthamstow** or **Deptford**, have begun to host independent stays in former textile factories and community buildings. These places don't just offer beds; they invite you into local stories. When the owner tells you how the building once stored hops for a nearby brewery or how an artist designed the tiles in the hallway, you're not just hearing history — you're living inside it.

Choosing such accommodation isn't about luxury; it's about memory. Long after you've returned home, you may forget the view from your window, but you won't forget how it *felt* to stay somewhere that mattered.

3. Sleep Among History: Unusual Stays in Former Schools, Churches, and Pubs

London's past isn't trapped in museums — sometimes, you can literally sleep inside it. Have you ever stayed in a building that once served a completely different purpose? A place where you can almost feel the echoes of other lives? This city is full of such spaces that have been thoughtfully turned into one-of-a-kind accommodations.

Imagine checking into a **former Victorian schoolhouse** where chalkboards remain on the walls, or staying in a **converted church** where stained-glass windows scatter soft light across your bed in the morning. These aren't gimmicks — they're living pieces of heritage reimagined for travelers who want something real.

Many of London's old **pubs** have also found second lives as boutique inns. Picture rooms upstairs where weary travelers once stayed after long coach rides, now polished but still full of character. Downstairs, locals gather for pints, quiz nights, and laughter — and you get to be part of it.

In **Clerkenwell**, you'll find historic printworks turned into minimalist apartments. In **Shoreditch**, there are stays inside old textile mills that whisper of the East End's working-class roots. Every brick seems to hold a story, and staying there lets you feel the continuity between past and present.

These unusual accommodations remind us that travel isn't only about what you see outside — it's about what surrounds you when you close the door at night. Why settle for generic when you could wake up in a building that has seen centuries unfold?

4. Choosing the Right Area for Hidden Discoveries

Selecting the right neighborhood can completely change your trip. Many first-time visitors rush to stay near Westminster or Oxford Street, thinking proximity means practicality. But have you ever noticed how being "close to everything" often means being "surrounded by everyone"? The charm of London lives in the spaces where you can breathe, listen, and notice the small things — a vintage bookshop, a Sunday market, or a café filled with locals.

So, how do you choose? Think about your travel rhythm. Do you enjoy peaceful mornings or lively nights? Do you prefer independent shops over high-street brands? Here's a simple way to decide:

- If you want **quiet beauty**, stay near **Hampstead** or **Greenwich**. You'll get leafy walks, heritage buildings, and calm evenings.
- For **creative energy**, try **Shoreditch**, **Hackney**, or **Peckham**, where art meets food in every corner.
- If you crave **historic charm**, explore **Clerkenwell**, **Bloomsbury**, or **Spitalfields**, where you'll walk on cobblestones that have stories to tell.

Don't be afraid of a short train or bus ride. London's transport network is one of the best in the world, and staying slightly away from the main hubs can give you access to areas most tourists never touch. Sometimes, the extra 15 minutes it takes to get "home" means you'll return to peace, not crowds.

The best stays often sit on the edge of discovery — close enough to explore, far enough to feel authentic.

5. *Mistake to Avoid:* **Staying Too Central and Missing the Real London**

It's easy to believe that being central means being connected. But the truth? Staying too close to the tourist core can make your experience feel repetitive. Every restaurant serves similar menus, every shop sells the same souvenirs, and the soundtrack of your trip becomes the buzz of traffic rather than the hum of local life.

The heart of London beats strongest in its outer neighborhoods — where markets spill onto pavements, where people still greet each other by name, where pubs double as community centers. Have you ever wandered through an area where no one is taking photos, yet every corner feels like a discovery? That's the experience you risk missing if you confine yourself to the center.

When you step just a few Underground stops further out, you start to see the city's real variety. You'll find Turkish bakeries in Dalston, Portuguese cafés in Stockwell, Caribbean grocers in Brixton, and family-owned Italian delis in Crouch End. Each one offers a piece of the city's enormous cultural puzzle — pieces you'd never find near Leicester Square.

So before booking, pause for a moment. Ask yourself what you want your memories to look like. Do you want a view of Big Ben from a hotel window, or do you want to share breakfast with locals in a family-run café tucked behind a park?

London rewards curiosity. Its magic lies not only in its grand monuments but in the quiet corners most visitors never see. Choosing where to stay isn't just logistics; it's an invitation — to see the city differently, to slow down, to feel part of the stories that live in its side streets. The best stays don't just offer a place to sleep; they open a door to the kind of experiences that make you fall in love with the city itself.

When you choose carefully, you stop being a visitor and start living like someone who belongs — even if it's just for a few days. And isn't that what travel should truly be about?

CHAPTeR 4

LONDON'S STORY BENEATH THE SURFACE

Every great city hides something. In London, what lies beneath the noise and neon is not just history—it's a living, breathing reminder of how time keeps moving while traces of the past cling to its bricks, tunnels, and narrow lanes. People walk over centuries every single day without realizing it. Have you ever wondered what stories linger beneath your feet as you cross Westminster Bridge or hurry through King's Cross Station? If the streets could speak, what would they say?

Most visitors come to London with a checklist—Big Ben, the London Eye, Buckingham Palace. But the real heart of the city beats in places no guidebook map will show you. The forgotten tunnels, hidden courtyards, and fading street signs tell stories that shaped the London we see today. The aim of this chapter is simple: to guide you through the unseen, to help you slow down and notice what most people pass by. Because London's truest charm isn't found in postcards—it's hidden beneath your footsteps.

1. Layers of Time: The City's Forgotten Eras and Overlooked Heroes

London has lived through everything—Roman conquest, plague, fire, war, and rebirth. But it's easy to forget that behind every famous landmark, there are invisible layers of history. The Roman walls that once marked the city's limits still peek through in quiet corners near the Tower. Medieval lanes twist behind modern glass offices. Georgian terraces stand beside Victorian warehouses. The city is like a living timeline, built one story on top of another.

Yet, the people who shaped those stories often fade from memory. Take the Thames lightermen, for example—the men who ferried goods across the river for centuries, navigating fog, ice, and tides long before modern bridges. Or the "mudlarks," children and scavengers who once picked through river sludge to survive. They rarely make it into guidebooks, yet without them, London would never have grown into the hub it became.

It's worth pausing to ask yourself: when you walk through Covent Garden or Spitalfields, whose footsteps are you following? The answer might surprise you. Beneath the boutiques and cafés, these were once places of hard labour, trade, and survival. The scent of spices at the docks, the clang of blacksmiths in Soho, the chatter of market sellers in East End alleys—all echoes of forgotten lives that shaped modern London.

To explore these layers, slow down. Visit the Museum of London Docklands to see the city's working past up close. Wander through Leadenhall Market, where Roman ruins lie just a few feet below your path. And when you pass an old plaque or weathered street sign, stop and read it. Each one is a whisper from another time.

2. Underground History: Abandoned Tube Stations and Hidden Tunnels

Few cities can claim an underground story as fascinating as London's. The Tube is the oldest underground railway in the world, but beneath it lie other tunnels—some forgotten, some sealed, some still holding secrets. Ever heard of Aldwych Station? It's been closed since 1994 but often used for film shoots and secret tours. Its tiled corridors still carry the ghosts of wartime passengers who sheltered there during the Blitz.

Then there's Down Street Station, once part of the Piccadilly line. During World War II, it became Winston Churchill's private bunker. Imagine hearing air raid sirens above while decisions that shaped history were being made below. Today, London Transport Museum occasionally opens it to the public, giving visitors a rare glimpse into the city's wartime underground life.

But not all tunnels are part of the Tube. Beneath the streets lie forgotten rivers like the Fleet, Tyburn, and Walbrook—now hidden within sewers and drains. Centuries ago, they flowed through open air, shaping the city's layout. In some parts of Clerkenwell or Holborn, you can still hear water rushing under the pavement after a heavy rain.

The tunnels tell us something powerful about Londoners: they adapt. They build new layers over the old but never erase them completely. Exploring these hidden spaces helps you understand that every era leaves its mark—and some never fully disappear.

If you're adventurous, join a guided tour with Hidden London, an official program that grants access to disused stations. You'll walk corridors frozen in time, see posters from decades ago, and feel the eerie calm of spaces that once buzzed with life.

3. Secret Architecture: Mews, Courtyards, and Lost Villages

London's beauty isn't only in its grand landmarks—it hides in quiet corners, in the unexpected stillness between busy streets. Ever turned down a narrow lane in Kensington and suddenly found yourself in a cobbled mews lined with ivy-covered stables? These mews once housed horses and carriages for the wealthy; now, they're among the city's most charming addresses.

The courtyards of Bloomsbury and Holborn, tucked between old buildings, feel like time capsules. Red brick walls, wrought-iron gates, and the faint sound of footsteps echoing between offices—it's where old London breathes quietly. Lincoln's Inn Fields, for instance, offers a peaceful escape where barristers once debated cases beneath plane trees that have stood for centuries.

And then there are the lost villages—places that were once separate hamlets, now absorbed by the growing city. Hampstead, Highgate, and Dulwich still keep their village feel, with local pubs, narrow lanes, and centuries-old houses. You might forget you're even in the capital. In Hampstead, the winding backstreets near Flask Walk still hold a quiet charm untouched by modernity.

Why do these places matter? Because they remind us that London wasn't built in a day—it grew through layers of human life, one courtyard and cobblestone at a time. These spaces offer something every traveler craves: a moment of discovery. A sense that you've found something personal, something that doesn't belong on a map.

The best way to find them? Wander without a plan. Let curiosity lead. Step off Oxford Street and into Marylebone Lane, or slip behind Covent Garden Market into Neal's Yard, where color bursts from every wall. You'll see the London that locals love but rarely talk about—the one that feels almost secret.

4. The City Within a City: The Secrets of the Square Mile

The Square Mile, London's ancient financial district, might look like a maze of glass towers and suits today, but underneath that modern shine lies one of the oldest corners of the city. This was once the Roman settlement of Londinium. Its boundaries are still marked by fragments of the old wall that once protected the city from invaders.

Most people rush through this area on business, never noticing the quiet courtyards, old churches, and narrow alleys that crisscross between skyscrapers. Places like St. Dunstan in the East—a bombed-out church now turned into a tranquil garden—offer rare calm in the heart of the city. Then there's Postman's Park, where a memorial honors ordinary people who died performing acts of bravery. It's humbling, silent, and easy to miss unless you're looking.

The City also hides its own underground history. Under Guildhall lies a Roman amphitheatre, once the stage for public games. You can visit it today, hidden beneath modern floors. And in the shadow of St. Paul's, you'll find streets like Wardrobe Place and Carter Lane—names that recall the trades and stories of centuries past.

Think of the Square Mile as London's memory vault. Everything that defines the city—commerce, resilience, reinvention—started here. When you walk through it, take a moment to look up and down. Between the glass and steel, you'll see pieces of stone that have witnessed nearly 2,000 years of history.

Local Secret: **The Smallest Museum in London You've Never Heard Of**

If you think museums have to be grand, think again. Tucked between buildings on Brooks Mews in Mayfair sits one of London's tiniest treasures—the Fan Museum? No. The smallest one is actually the **Kirkaldy Testing Museum** or even smaller: the **Westminster Fire Brigade Museum**, but there's another even lesser-known gem—the **Traffic Light Tree miniature exhibit**, or the **Cartoon Museum's secret annex**. Yet, the one that often surprises visitors most is **The Smallest Police Station in Trafalgar Square**, a one-person box carved into a lamp post.

Though technically not a museum, it stands as a reminder of London's love for hidden curiosities. Just big enough for one officer, it was once used to monitor protests. Most people pass it daily without realizing its history. It's a perfect example of how London hides its quirks in plain sight.

If you want an actual "smallest museum," head to the **Tiny Museum of Brands in Notting Hill**—a private collection of everyday packaging and adverts that trace British life through the decades. It's a nostalgic, charming look at how culture changes over time—proof that even the smallest spaces can hold big stories.

To understand London, you need to do more than look—you need to *notice*. Every corner, every tunnel, every mews lane holds a clue to who Londoners were and who they are today. The city doesn't shout about its past; it whispers. The joy comes from listening carefully.

So next time you walk its streets, pause. Look closer at the cracks in the pavement, the old lettering on a shop sign, the quiet lane between two busy roads. Because somewhere beneath all that noise and movement, London is still telling its story—layer by layer, waiting for someone curious enough to hear it.

Chapter 5

Food with a Local Twist: Eating Beyond the Usual

There's something magical about discovering a city through its food. Not the polished, picture-perfect meals you find in fancy restaurants, but the ones that tell stories — meals cooked by families, shared between friends, and served in places that don't always make it onto glossy travel lists. London's food scene has a heartbeat of its own, pulsing through backstreets, hidden courtyards, and cozy corners that only locals seem to know. If you've ever thought London was all about afternoon tea and fish and chips, think again. The real adventure begins when you start eating beyond the usual.

Most travelers arrive in London ready to tick off the famous spots — a pub lunch near Big Ben, maybe dinner at a Michelin-starred restaurant, or a quick bite from a trendy food hall. But the question is — what happens when you step away from the guidebook recommendations? What if you let your appetite lead you through the city's hidden doors and unexpected flavors? That's where London becomes unforgettable.

This chapter is about that very experience — discovering the side of London that locals taste every day. From tucked-away markets that still smell of freshly baked bread and roasted coffee to small family-run kitchens that serve recipes passed down for generations, this is your invitation to eat like a Londoner. We'll explore where to find them, how to spot the good ones, and what makes these places worth your time.

1. Hidden Markets and Tiny Cafés That Locals Love

The best meals in London rarely come from the places with long queues or fancy menus. They come from markets tucked behind narrow lanes and cafés that look so ordinary you might walk past them without a second glance. These are the places where the city's food culture thrives quietly — places that locals return to week after week because they trust what's on the plate.

Think about this: how often do you find yourself in a new city, surrounded by options, but unsure of where to eat without falling into a tourist trap? London can be the same, but locals have a trick — they follow the smells and the crowds of regulars who seem to know exactly where they're going.

Take Maltby Street Market in Bermondsey, for instance. It's smaller than the famous Borough Market, but it's where Londoners actually go when they crave good food without the fuss. You can find everything from slow-cooked beef brisket sandwiches dripping with sauce to handmade doughnuts stuffed with fresh jam. There's laughter, the sound of sizzling pans, and the comfort of knowing every stall has a story.

Or wander to Exmouth Market in Clerkenwell. Here, between small design shops and bookshops, you'll find cafés that seem to exist in their own time zone. A tiny Italian café serving perfect espresso and warm focaccia. A Syrian bakery selling flaky pastries filled with pistachio. It's not fancy — it's familiar, warm, and exactly what locals love.

The secret? Don't rush. Sit down. Talk to the people behind the counter. Ask what's good that day — and don't be surprised if they offer you something not on the menu. That's how you discover London's hidden flavors.

2. Family-Run Restaurants and Pop-Ups in Unexpected Places

Every London neighborhood has at least one spot where locals swear by the food, even if it's hidden behind a row of houses or under a railway arch. These are often family-run restaurants that started with one dream — to share their culture's food with whoever walks in.

Imagine finding a Sri Lankan curry house in a quiet part of Tooting, where the owner still greets every guest personally and remembers your order from last week. Or a tiny Cypriot restaurant in Harringay, where you'll eat grilled halloumi and lamb kebabs while the owner's mother cooks in the back kitchen.

Pop-ups are another part of London's food magic. They appear in the most unexpected places — on rooftops, inside old warehouses, or even in someone's backyard. These are run by passionate chefs who want to experiment and share their ideas with the city. One month you might find a ramen stall run by a Japanese student perfecting his grandmother's recipe. The next, a Venezuelan arepa stand that disappears after three weekends but leaves behind a loyal following.

Here's the thing about these places — they remind you that food doesn't have to be perfect to be memorable. It just has to be real. And in London, authenticity doesn't come from fine dining. It comes from people who cook from memory, who believe that a meal should make you feel something.

3. Historic Pubs, Secret Bars, and Rooftop Hideaways

Nowhere tells the story of London better than its pubs. They're not just places to drink — they're community living rooms. Some have been around for centuries, their wooden beams darkened by time, their floors creaking under stories of laughter, love, and late-night songs.

Step inside The Seven Stars near the Royal Courts of Justice — one of the city's oldest pubs — and you'll find yourself surrounded by wigs, robes, and history. The pub's cat, wearing a ruff, might even greet you at the door. Or wander into The Prospect of Whitby in Wapping, a riverside pub dating back to the 1500s, where pirates once drank. Sit by the window and watch the Thames roll by as you sip a pint and imagine the stories that have unfolded there.

But London's hidden corners also shine after dark in more modern ways. Behind unmarked doors and dimly lit staircases, secret bars and speakeasies wait to be found. In Shoreditch, a fridge door inside a sandwich shop leads to one of the city's most creative cocktail lounges. In Soho, a tiny jazz bar hides under a record store — no signs, no fuss, just pure atmosphere.

And when the sun sets over the skyline, head to a rooftop that locals keep to themselves. The Culpeper in Spitalfields grows its own herbs and vegetables for the kitchen on its rooftop garden, offering views of London that most visitors never see. These are the moments that make you feel part of the city — not just visiting it.

4. The London You Can Taste: Street Food with a Story

Street food is London at its boldest. It's loud, colorful, and full of surprises. Every bite tells a story — sometimes of migration, sometimes of innovation, always of passion.

At Camden Market, you'll find food from every corner of the planet. But look closer and you'll see it's not just about variety — it's about identity. The Jamaican jerk stand run by a father and daughter who learned the recipe from their grandmother. The Polish pierogi stall where every dumpling is handmade. The Ethiopian coffee hut where the owner roasts beans on-site, filling the air with the most inviting smell you'll ever experience.

If you want something more local, visit Broadway Market in Hackney on a Saturday morning. It's where the neighborhood comes alive with food, music, and laughter. Grab a sausage roll from a baker who's been there for twenty years, or try vegan tacos that taste so good you'll forget they're vegan.

Street food in London isn't about eating fast — it's about eating freely. No reservations, no rules. You eat standing up, surrounded by strangers who are also smiling because they've just discovered something good. And that's what makes it special — every meal feels like a small celebration.

5. *Insider Tip:* Where Chefs Eat on Their Day Off

Here's a truth that most visitors never hear — if you want to find the best food in any city, go where the chefs go on their day off. In London, that means skipping the trendy spots and heading for the simple ones that serve honest, comforting meals.

You might find a Michelin-starred chef eating ramen at Bone Daddies in Soho, or grabbing dumplings in Chinatown at midnight. Many head to Dishoom for a plate of spicy breakfast eggs and endless chai, or to Koya for handmade udon noodles so good they taste like home.

Why do they choose these places? Because they serve food that feels personal — meals cooked with heart, not just skill. And that's the secret you should remember as you explore London's hidden food scene.

Don't chase the reviews. Follow the aromas, the laughter, the lines of locals who don't check menus before ordering. Those are the signs that you're about to find something worth remembering.

London doesn't reveal its best flavors right away. It rewards curiosity — the kind that makes you peek down a narrow alley or step into a café that looks too small to notice. When you start to explore this way, food becomes more than fuel. It becomes a story — one that connects you to the people, the city, and maybe even a new part of yourself.

So next time you're hungry in London, don't ask, "Where should I eat?" Ask instead, "What story do I want to taste today?" Because in this city, the best meals aren't always found — they're discovered.

Chapter 6

Neighborhood Secrets: The Soul of the Hidden City

Where London's True Spirit Lives

Every traveler thinks they know London. The red buses, Big Ben, the buzzing markets. But if you stop for a moment, you'll realize the city's true heartbeat doesn't echo through the landmarks — it hums quietly through its neighborhoods. The real London lives in the hidden corners, on quiet lanes, and behind unassuming doors where locals shop, laugh, and tell stories that never make it to the guidebooks.

This chapter is your key to that secret world. You'll explore neighborhoods that hold the soul of London — places where creativity, history, and community blend into something unforgettable. Whether you're a first-time visitor or a returning explorer, you'll soon see why locals never stop discovering new sides of their own city.

1. North London: Secret Gardens of Hampstead & Railway Bridges of Camden

If you've ever thought London was all noise, traffic, and rushing commuters, North London quietly disagrees. Behind the busy streets and red buses, it hides corners that most visitors never stumble upon. Have you ever wondered what the city looks like when it slows down—when it takes a breath? North London is where that happens.

Start with Hampstead. Many know about Hampstead Heath, but few step into the secret gardens tucked behind high hedges and narrow lanes. Some are attached to old Georgian homes, others belong to artists' studios or quiet community plots where locals grow herbs and wildflowers. You can wander through Church Row or Flask Walk and catch glimpses of ivy climbing up weathered brick walls, or the flash of a cat leaping across a garden gate. Every turn feels like a secret shared only with you.

One of the most peaceful corners is the Hampstead Hill Garden and Pergola—a raised walkway covered in vines, overlooking a sunken garden that feels lost in time. Many Londoners have lived their whole lives without visiting it. Can you imagine that? Standing there, surrounded by wisteria and whispers of old conversations, you begin to see why locals treasure this side of the city.

Then, shift toward Camden—but not the Camden you've seen in postcards filled with neon signs and music stalls. Cross under the railway bridges and head toward the old industrial backstreets, where time feels slower. These iron and brick arches have become homes to artists, craft brewers, and small independent workshops. Street art decorates the walls, and if you pause, you might hear the soft hum of live music escaping from a tucked-away studio.

What makes this part of London special isn't what's on display—it's what hides in plain sight. It's in the conversations between stallholders, in the scent of coffee roasting beneath railway tracks, and in the laughter echoing through old warehouses that refuse to fade. Want to feel the heartbeat of North London? Step off the main path and follow the sound of creativity—it's everywhere, if you're paying attention.

2. East London: Street Art Alleys and Old Warehouses Turned Galleries

If North London feels like an old secret, East London is a bold whisper. It's where the city's edge meets its imagination. The streets here tell stories not through words, but through color, murals, and the layers of paint that mark decades of change. Have you ever looked at a wall and realized it's holding history? That's what East London does best.

In Shoreditch, every alley is an outdoor gallery. Walk down Brick Lane, and you'll find murals that change almost weekly—portraits of protest, humor, and heartbreak. Each artist leaves a mark, and another builds on it. It's messy, yes, but it's also alive. This isn't art meant for galleries with velvet ropes—it's art that breathes the same air as the street vendors and passersby.

Beyond the graffiti, the old warehouses tell another story. These vast industrial spaces once stored fabrics and machinery; now they hold creativity. Many have been transformed into art studios, performance spaces, and design workshops. A century ago, people worked here to survive. Today, people work here to express. It's transformation you can feel as soon as you walk in.

But here's the real secret: not every hidden spot is marked on a map. Sometimes it's a door half-covered in posters, leading to a rooftop where local photographers meet. Sometimes it's a narrow lane near Hackney Wick that opens into a riverside bar with mismatched furniture and fairy lights. The joy of East London is in the discovery. You don't need a guide—just curiosity and good shoes.

If you want to connect with the city's creative pulse, spend an afternoon exploring without a plan. Follow the sound of buskers under Shoreditch High Street station. Peek inside pop-up galleries where the art might disappear tomorrow. East London reminds you that beauty doesn't last forever—it's meant to be found, appreciated, and remembered before it changes again.

3. South London: Dulwich Lanes, Forest Hill Cafés & Crystal Palace Ruins

South London often feels like the part of the city that guards its mysteries. Tourists rarely cross the river unless it's for Greenwich or the London Eye—but those who do discover something different. Have you ever walked through a neighborhood that feels both urban and rural at once? That's the charm of the south.

Start in Dulwich. Its narrow lanes, lined with cottages and trees, lead you to quiet green spaces and small galleries like the Dulwich Picture Gallery—the oldest public art gallery in England. But the real treasure lies just behind those main paths. Wander past the hidden mews and small courtyards, and you'll find garden cafés where locals read newspapers and share homemade cakes. It's London with the volume turned down.

Forest Hill and Sydenham have their own kind of magic too. The Horniman Museum, with its quirky collection of instruments and taxidermy, sits high on a hill with views stretching across the city. But beyond the museum grounds, small independent cafés and thrift shops line the streets, creating an atmosphere that feels personal and lived-in. These are the places where you strike up conversations with strangers who quickly feel like neighbors.

And then there's Crystal Palace—named for a building that no longer stands, but whose ruins still whisper stories. Walk through Crystal Palace Park and you'll find strange Victorian dinosaur sculptures, hidden lakes, and overgrown paths that make you feel like an explorer in your own city. The park's layout mirrors old grandeur, but today it feels like nature reclaiming history. How often can you say you've walked through a park where both dinosaurs and time seem to have paused?

South London's hidden corners remind you that the city's best treasures don't need big signs. They ask you to look closer, to notice the details others overlook—the smell of fresh bread from a small bakery, the street musician playing for no one in particular, the faded plaque on a forgotten wall.

4. West London: Notting Hill's Quiet Streets and Hammersmith's Riverside Corners

When people think of West London, they imagine pastel houses and the buzz of Portobello Market. But what if you wandered a few blocks away from the crowds? Would you find a London that feels softer, slower, and more personal? The answer is yes—and it's more beautiful than most imagine.

Notting Hill, famous for its color and energy, has another side. Behind the rows of busy market stalls, quiet streets stretch out, lined with old townhouses and climbing roses. Walk early in the morning or late in the afternoon, and you'll catch the light bouncing off pastel facades, with no one else around. Some of these streets, like St. Luke's Mews or Colville Terrace, feel frozen in time—more like scenes from a film than real life. Yet they are real, lived-in, and loved.

Hammersmith, too, has a gentler secret. The Thames Path here reveals riverside pubs, tiny boat clubs, and benches shaded by willows. Locals come for quiet walks, morning runs, or evening reflections. You can sit by the river, watch the rowers glide past, and feel the city fade into calm. There's something almost meditative about it—a reminder that even in one of the world's busiest capitals, stillness exists if you know where to look.

For a real hidden gem, wander through Ravenscourt Park, just nearby. Most visitors miss it entirely, yet it's one of West London's most peaceful spots. You'll find duck ponds, winding trails, and locals walking their dogs, far from the tourist rush.

West London whispers rather than shouts. It offers moments— quiet gardens, riverside walks, a small café on a corner where the staff greet you like family. And if you listen carefully, you'll realize that these are the parts of the city that make people fall in love with it—not the landmarks, but the life between them.

Local Secret: The Neighborhoods Londoners Don't Tell Tourists About

Ask a Londoner for their favorite spot, and chances are they'll hesitate. Not because they don't have one—but because they don't want it crowded. Every local has their own corner of the city that feels like it belongs only to them. Maybe it's a canal-side bench in Maida Vale, a backstreet curry house in Tooting, or a hidden rooftop in Dalston. These are the places that don't make it to travel guides or influencer reels. They survive because they stay secret.

So how do you find them? The trick isn't in maps or blogs—it's in your pace. Walk slower. Talk to people. Take wrong turns. Visit local markets early in the morning when vendors are still setting up. Step inside independent bookshops and ask the staff what café they love nearby. Most of London's secrets reveal themselves when you stop trying to "see everything" and start experiencing something.

You might discover a record shop that doubles as a bar, a back-alley cinema with mismatched chairs, or a tiny park between apartment blocks that bursts with cherry blossoms in spring. Each corner tells its own quiet story, and together they form the heartbeat of the city.

The hidden side of London isn't just about finding places others miss—it's about finding your own version of the city. The one that matches your pace, your curiosity, your way of seeing. Because the truth is, London doesn't have one soul—it has millions. The question is, which one will you find first?

CHAPTeR 7

TiME TRAVEL — HiddEN HiSTORiC ANd CULTURAL SiTES OF LONdON

Have you ever walked down a quiet London street and wondered what secrets lie behind its old walls? Beneath the city's polished landmarks and busy attractions are forgotten treasures—places that hold echoes of kings, artists, and dreamers long gone. This chapter takes you on a different kind of London journey. Not through the tourist-filled streets, but through time itself—into corners of history that few visitors ever see.

If you've ever felt that popular landmarks tell only part of the story, you're right. The real magic of London lies in the hidden details—the churches built on Roman ruins, the crypts where centuries whisper through the stone, the forgotten palaces that shaped the aristocracy, and the small museums that carry enormous cultural legacies. This chapter will help you uncover those hidden gems, understand their meaning, and experience London the way true locals and historians do.

1. Lesser-Known Churches, Crypts, and Cemeteries

When people visit London, they often rush to St. Paul's Cathedral or Westminster Abbey. But beyond these grand icons lie small chapels and centuries-old cemeteries that reveal London's spiritual and social history in a deeper, quieter way.

Take **St. Dunstan-in-the-East**, for example. Once a medieval church destroyed during the Blitz, it now stands as a hauntingly beautiful public garden. Ivy climbs the ruined arches, and sunlight filters through open windows where stained glass once stood. It's peaceful, poetic—and free.

Then there's **Postman's Park**, a hidden memorial near St. Paul's that honors ordinary people who died saving others. Each plaque tells a moving story of courage—ordinary Londoners turned heroes. It's a reminder that history isn't just about kings and queens; it's also about compassion.

Don't miss **Bunhill Fields Cemetery**, where writers like William Blake and Daniel Defoe rest. It's quiet and full of symbolism. Walking there feels like stepping into the mind of London's literary past.

Tip: Visit early in the morning for stillness. Bring a notebook— you might find yourself inspired to write.

2. Small Museums with Big Stories

London is filled with massive museums like the British Museum or the National Gallery, but the soul of the city often hides in its smaller, lesser-known ones. These places tell stories that larger institutions overlook.

For example, **The Foundling Museum** tells the story of abandoned children in 18th-century London and the man who gave them a future, Thomas Coram. The art, music, and personal letters on display create an emotional journey through a forgotten part of social history.

Then there's **The Hunterian Museum**, a fascinating collection of medical instruments and anatomical specimens that once shaped the future of science. It's both eerie and enlightening.

Another gem is **The Museum of Brands** in Notting Hill. Here, packaging and advertisements from the Victorian era to today reveal how British culture evolved—through chocolate bars, soaps, and cereals.

Tip: Choose one or two small museums per day. Their size lets you slow down, absorb details, and truly connect with the past.

3. Forgotten Palaces and Gardens of the Aristocracy

London's grand palaces—like Buckingham or Kensington—attract crowds. But scattered across the city are smaller estates that once hosted the aristocracy, now quietly fading into history.

Eltham Palace, for example, is part medieval, part Art Deco masterpiece. Once a royal residence and later redesigned by millionaires Stephen and Virginia Courtauld, it perfectly blends two eras—old tapestries meet sleek 1930s design.

Then there's **Syon House**, the London home of the Duke of Northumberland. It's one of the best-preserved examples of Robert Adam's neoclassical architecture. The interiors alone could tell a thousand stories of noble ambition and changing tastes.

And for something truly enchanting, stroll through **Holland Park's Kyoto Garden**—a peaceful Japanese garden gifted to London in the 1990s. Though not aristocratic in origin, it carries the same sense of cultivated beauty that once defined noble estates.

Tip: Many of these sites offer combined tickets or heritage passes—ideal for slow travelers who want to explore over several days.

4. Theatres, Record Shops, and Studios That Shaped London's Art Scene

London's creative pulse has always been strong, but not all its artistic landmarks are in the spotlight. Some of its most revolutionary art, music, and theatre came from tiny venues and modest studios that changed history.

Visit **The Old Operating Theatre Museum** near London Bridge—not exactly a theatre in the modern sense, but one of Europe's oldest surviving surgical theatres. It's a place where performance met medicine, where crowds once gathered to watch early surgeries in awe and fear.

For music lovers, **Rough Trade East** in Brick Lane is more than a record shop—it's a symbol of rebellion. Since the 1970s, it's been a meeting point for independent artists and fans of punk, rock, and alternative music.

And if you walk through **Soho**, you'll find old recording studios like **Trident Studios**, where David Bowie, Queen, and Elton John recorded. Even if you can't go inside, knowing what happened behind those brick walls makes your walk feel like a pilgrimage.

Tip: Pair your visit with a live show at a small venue like **The Old Red Lion Theatre** or **The Almeida**. These are where tomorrow's legends are born.

5. Mistake to Avoid: Visiting the Big Landmarks First

It's easy to start your trip with the famous spots—Tower of London, Buckingham Palace, Big Ben. But here's the problem: once you've seen the big names, smaller sites can feel "less exciting" in comparison. You lose the patience and curiosity that make hidden gems magical.

Instead, **reverse your itinerary**. Start with the hidden places first. Let the smaller stories build your connection to the city. Then, when you finally visit the major landmarks, you'll see them differently—with context, understanding, and appreciation.

Tip: Create your own "secret London" map. Add one hidden site for every famous attraction you plan to visit. It keeps your journey balanced and full of surprises.

Exploring hidden historic and cultural sites isn't just about sightseeing—it's about **time travel**. Each small church, forgotten palace, or quiet museum is a doorway into another era. You'll come away not just with photos, but with a deeper sense of London's living history.

By taking the time to explore what others overlook, you discover the real heart of the city—a place shaped by faith, creativity, and resilience. The more you wander off the map, the more you'll understand why London isn't just a place to visit—it's a story to live.

CHAPTeR 8

SEASONS IN THE SHADOWS: WHEN TO EXPLORE

Every city has its secrets—but London hides them best. Beyond the usual tourist paths, the city transforms with each season, revealing a different side of itself. There are moments when the air smells of cherry blossoms, times when the streets glow golden under autumn light, and days when fog wraps hidden corners in quiet magic. This chapter is your guide to discovering London's secret side, season by season—when crowds thin, when the mood shifts, and when you can truly feel the city breathe.

1. London in Spring: Secret Gardens and Blossom Walks

Spring in London feels like the city is waking from a long dream. Streets that were gray in winter suddenly burst into pinks and whites. For many travelers, the challenge is knowing where to see this softer side of London without bumping shoulders with hundreds of others doing the same.

The Problem:

Most visitors head straight for the obvious—Kew Gardens, Hyde Park, or Regent's Park. Beautiful, yes—but they can be crowded. The magic lies in the quieter spots, where cherry blossoms fall without interruption and gardens whisper instead of shout.

The Solution:

Explore hidden gardens and lesser-known lanes. Start with St. Dunstan in the East, a ruined church turned garden near the Tower of London. Its ivy-covered walls and quiet benches feel worlds away from the busy city. Then head to Postman's Park, tucked between office buildings near St. Paul's Cathedral, where memorial tablets tell forgotten stories of heroism.

In South Kensington, wander to Kensington Roof Gardens or the Chelsea Physic Garden, one of the oldest botanical gardens in Britain. In Greenwich, the Queen's Orchard blooms with apple and pear blossoms that look like scenes from a fairy tale.

Actionable Tips:

- Visit early in the morning when the light is soft and the paths are empty.
- Bring a small sketchbook or camera to capture the seasonal colors.
- Avoid weekends if possible—weekday mornings are perfect.

Pro Tip: Combine a garden walk with a visit to a local café. Spring in London pairs beautifully with tea, pastel macarons, and window seats overlooking cobblestone streets.

2. Summer Escapes: Quiet Parks and Hidden Rooftops

When the summer sun shines on London, the city changes tempo. Everyone wants to be outdoors—but not everyone wants the crowds of Hyde Park or the chaos of Covent Garden. The challenge is finding peace in the midst of the buzz.

The Problem:

London in summer can feel overwhelming. Tourists fill the parks, queues grow longer, and many travelers crave an escape that still feels authentically London.

The Solution:

Head to Hampstead Pergola and Hill Gardens. Overgrown wisteria and stone archways make it one of the city's dreamiest summer spots. Few tourists know it exists. Then, cool down in Little Venice, where canal boats drift slowly under willow trees.

If you crave views without the crowds, skip the Sky Garden and visit The Culpeper Rooftop Garden in Spitalfields. It's a working garden and restaurant offering herbs, cocktails, and sunset views over East London's rooftops.

For a slower pace, wander through Holland Park's Kyoto Garden, where koi fish and waterfalls create quiet harmony.

Actionable Tips:

- Visit rooftops during "golden hour" (about 7–8 p.m.) for fewer crowds and stunning photos.
- Pack a lightweight blanket for spontaneous picnics.
- Always carry sunscreen—London surprises with sun!

Pro Tip: Book a weekday table at a hidden rooftop bar in Shoreditch or Peckham before sunset. You'll see London at its best—bathed in warm light, alive but calm.

3. Autumn Discoveries: Leafy Lanes and Candlelit Pubs

Autumn is when London turns poetic. Leaves fall like confetti, the air smells of roasted chestnuts, and the city feels nostalgic. It's the season of reflection, quiet walks, and cozy corners.

The Problem:

Most travelers overlook London in autumn, thinking the best time to visit is summer. Yet, autumn offers cheaper stays, fewer crowds, and a richer atmosphere—if you know where to go.

The Solution:

Start in Richmond Park, where ancient oaks and free-roaming deer set the scene for peaceful walks. Wander through Hampstead Heath, especially Parliament Hill, for golden views of the skyline. Then head to Primrose Hill—the sunset colors over the city are unforgettable.

When the air grows colder, retreat to The Churchill Arms in Kensington or Ye Olde Cheshire Cheese near Fleet Street—pubs that glow with candlelight and old stories.

Actionable Tips:

- Visit parks just before sunset when light filters through the amber leaves.
- Bring a scarf and comfortable shoes—London's autumn weather shifts quickly.
- Try local dishes like steak and ale pie or sticky toffee pudding at small gastropubs.

Pro Tip: Don't rush. Autumn in London is about slowing down, watching leaves drift along the Thames, and savoring simple pleasures—a warm drink, soft music, and good company.

4. Winter Magic: Hidden Markets and Cozy Corners

Winter in London feels like stepping into a storybook. Fairy lights sparkle, markets hum with laughter, and hidden alleys glow under soft snow. It's romantic, peaceful, and unforgettable.

The Problem:

Many travelers assume winter in London means cold and gloom. But the truth is, this is when the city reveals its warmth—from its festive corners to its steaming cups of mulled wine.

The Solution:

Skip the crowds at Winter Wonderland and explore Maltby Street Market, a smaller, local food market with artisanal charm. Stroll through Leadenhall Market, where twinkling lights and Victorian architecture transport you to another era.

Warm up in Daunt Books in Marylebone or The Electric Cinema in Notting Hill—both perfect hideaways for cold afternoons.

Actionable Tips:

- Dress in layers; many shops and markets are heated.
- Carry gloves for outdoor markets and camera use.
- Visit after dark to enjoy London's festive lights—Oxford Street and Covent Garden are magical at night.

Pro Tip: Spend an evening in Coal Drops Yard at King's Cross, sipping hot chocolate under glowing arches while snowflakes fall around you.

5. Packing Note: What to Wear When Exploring Hidden Streets

London's weather can surprise you—rain, sun, and wind often share the same day. Dressing smartly means staying comfortable no matter the season.

Spring: Light layers, a rain jacket, and comfortable shoes for park walks.

Summer: Breathable fabrics, sunglasses, and a reusable water bottle.

Autumn: A warm sweater, waterproof boots, and a stylish scarf.

Winter: A thick coat, gloves, and something cozy for pub evenings.

Final Tip: Always carry a small umbrella—Londoners know it's the city's unofficial accessory.

London isn't just a city—it's a mood that changes with the seasons. Spring offers whispers of renewal, summer brings hidden joy, autumn wraps you in warmth, and winter glows with quiet magic. The best time to explore? Whenever your heart feels ready to see a new side of the old city.

Every season has its secret. All you have to do is walk slowly enough to find it.

CHAPTeR 9

Itineraries for Every Curious Traveler

Exploring a city is more than checking off landmarks—it's about feeling its pulse, hearing its whispers, and discovering its hidden corners that most people miss. Whether you have one day or a week, this chapter is your map to a more meaningful journey. Let's unlock experiences that reveal the soul of the city, not just its surface.

1. One Day: Quick Hidden Highlights

Imagine arriving with just twenty-four hours to spare. The challenge? Making every moment count without rushing. Most travelers flock to the main attractions, but what if your single day became a story worth telling—a day filled with unexpected corners, hidden cafes, and quiet charm?

Start your morning with a local breakfast spot where residents gather. Skip chain restaurants and ask for a café that serves the best homemade pastries or local coffee. Next, wander through a small park or garden—somewhere off the tourist radar but filled with life and calm.

By midday, visit a museum or gallery that rarely appears in guidebooks. These lesser-known places often tell stories the main exhibits forget—stories of local art, forgotten heroes, or unique traditions.

Spend your afternoon walking through narrow streets or local markets. Talk to vendors, sample regional snacks, and take in the everyday rhythm. Before sunset, find a quiet viewpoint. Watch the city glow as people head home, and let that be your closing chapter for the day.

Action Tip: Write down one thing that surprised you during your one-day trip. It could become your favorite travel memory.

2. Three Days: Explore the City's Overlooked Gems

Three days give you room to breathe—to balance famous sights with the secret ones. The problem many travelers face? They either overplan or wander without direction. The key is balance.

Day One can focus on the main highlights—the ones you feel you must see. This gives you a foundation and helps you understand the city's layout.

Day Two should be about discovery. Choose neighborhoods not found in most guidebooks—old industrial zones turned art spaces, local flea markets, or quiet bookshops with history. Take a walking tour led by a local guide who focuses on "hidden heritage" or "forgotten architecture."

Day Three is for reflection and rhythm. Visit a park or riverbank early in the morning. Observe the locals jogging, reading, or chatting. Have lunch at a family-run restaurant where recipes have stayed unchanged for generations. In the evening, attend a small local event—live music, poetry, or a craft workshop.

Expert Tip: Plan one "unknown" stop each day. Ask locals for their secret spot—you'll be surprised at what you discover.

3. A Week or More: Deep Dive into Local Life

A week allows you to go beyond the surface and into the heart of local life. You stop being a visitor and start becoming part of the city's rhythm. But here's the common mistake—many travelers treat a week as a checklist marathon. Instead, slow down.

Spend your mornings exploring and your afternoons living like a resident. Take public transport, shop at local markets, and greet the same barista each day. You'll start recognizing faces and feeling the warmth of familiarity.

Dedicate one or two days entirely to day trips. Visit surrounding villages, beaches, or countryside escapes that locals love but tourists rarely reach. These places often reveal authentic flavors, accents, and traditions.

In the evenings, join cooking classes, community meetups, or local film screenings. The more you connect, the deeper your understanding grows.

Checklist for a Week-Long Stay:

- Visit at least one major landmark for context.
- Discover three local-only gems.
- Learn one cultural skill (like cooking, art, or dance).
- Make one friend or personal connection.

4. Themed Trails: Secret Gardens, Forgotten Stations, Literary Corners

Some travelers love structure. Others crave stories. Themed trails combine both—they give purpose to your wandering. Instead of visiting random places, you follow a narrative.

Secret Gardens Trail: Hunt for hidden green spaces. Small courtyards, rooftop terraces, and community gardens often reveal quiet beauty and offer peaceful pauses.

Forgotten Stations Trail: Visit abandoned train platforms, historical depots, or vintage tram routes. Each holds echoes of a city's industrial past and resilience.

Literary Corners Trail: Follow the footsteps of local writers or famous books set in the city. Visit cafes they loved, libraries they frequented, and statues dedicated to their work.

Local Legends Trail: Explore spots tied to myths, ghost stories, or folk heroes. These add mystery and imagination to your journey.

Pro Tip: Choose one trail per trip. It creates focus while keeping exploration exciting and fresh.

5. Insider Tip: Mixing Popular and Hidden Spots for Balance

Every seasoned traveler knows the secret—balance is everything. Too many hidden places, and you might miss the city's spirit. Too many popular ones, and you blend into the crowd.

Plan your day like this: start with one famous landmark, follow with one hidden gem, then end with a relaxed local activity. For example, visit a famous cathedral in the morning, then explore a nearby independent art studio, and close the day with a meal at a local bistro.

This mix keeps your energy balanced and your memories rich. You'll see the best of both worlds—the celebrated and the secret.

Final Thought: True travel isn't about how much you see—it's about how deeply you connect. Whether you stay a day or a month, let curiosity guide you, not the crowd. The city will reveal itself in ways that only open-hearted travelers ever experience.

Chapter 10

Practical Wisdom for Urban Explorers

City Beyond the Guidebooks

Every city hides two versions of itself — the one tourists see and the one that quietly exists behind the noise. London is no different. Beyond its postcard landmarks, this city breathes through its backstreets, tiny cafés, and conversations overheard on park benches. But exploring off the beaten path isn't just about curiosity; it's about being smart, safe, and ready.

In this chapter, we'll walk through practical wisdom every urban explorer should know — how to stay safe while wandering, budget wisely, communicate respectfully, and use the right tools to connect with the real London. Think of this as your personal compass for the unseen city.

1. Staying Safe While Going Off the Beaten Path

Let's face it — adventure often starts where comfort ends. But safety should never be left behind. Exploring hidden corners of London means stepping into neighborhoods that might not be covered in your average guidebook. You'll find charm, character, and sometimes a few surprises — but being alert is key.

Start by trusting your instincts. If a street feels too quiet or isolated at night, don't test it. Choose to explore such areas during daylight hours. Keep your phone charged, location services on, and share your itinerary with a friend. In small cafés or local pubs, keep personal items close; London is safe, but like any major city, petty theft happens.

Public transport at night is reliable — but always check the route before heading out. Night buses and the Tube have CCTV and well-lit stations, but avoid empty carriages. When in doubt, call a licensed cab or use trusted ride-hailing apps like Bolt or Uber.

Quick Tips for Safe Exploration:

- Keep a small emergency contact card in your wallet.
- Download the "Citymapper" app to navigate without getting lost.
- Know where the nearest police or help point is.
- Dress like a local — blending in helps you feel confident and avoid unwanted attention.

Remember: exploring hidden places isn't about taking risks — it's about taking the right kind of care while doing something extraordinary.

2. Budgeting Smartly for Unique Experiences

One myth about London is that it's too expensive to enjoy deeply. That's only true if you explore like a tourist. Locals know that London rewards those who look closer — and think creatively about how they spend.

Start by setting a daily budget before you land. Then, divide it into essentials: food, transport, entry fees, and unexpected finds (like that irresistible secondhand bookshop in Notting Hill). The city offers countless free experiences — museums, galleries, street performances, and walking tours — that reveal just as much culture as paid attractions.

Smart Budget Moves:

- Buy an **Oyster Card** or use a contactless card for cheaper transport fares.
- Visit markets like **Maltby Street** or **Broadway Market** for local meals at half the restaurant price.

- Stay in a local guesthouse instead of a chain hotel — they're often cheaper and full of personality.
- Book theatre tickets on the day from discount booths or apps like "TodayTix."

A small secret? Londoners love value too. Many top restaurants offer fixed-price lunch menus — sometimes the same dishes at half the evening cost. Ask locals where they go. They'll usually point you toward hidden gems that don't appear on Google Maps.

Budgeting isn't about limiting fun — it's about opening space for spontaneous discoveries without guilt or worry.

3. Navigating Language, Etiquette, and Humor

Language in London isn't just English — it's expression, rhythm, and wit. Locals can tell if you're a traveler, but they'll warm up quickly if you understand their social cues.

Start with politeness. A simple "Sorry" or "Cheers" goes a long way. British manners may seem understated, but they're part of the city's unspoken language. Avoid speaking too loudly in quiet cafés or interrupting in queues — Londoners value personal space and patience.

Humor, however, is where you'll really connect. The British love irony, understatement, and self-deprecation. If someone jokes about the weather or a delayed train, it's their way of bonding, not complaining.

Cultural Navigation Tips:

- "You alright?" usually means "Hello," not a health check.
- Say "Thank you" often — it's appreciated.
- Avoid discussing politics or personal money matters unless invited.
- Learn a few Cockney rhyming phrases for fun — locals love it when you try.

Understanding these nuances will help you blend in, make friends, and experience a deeper, more authentic London — one that reveals itself only when you listen between the lines.

4. Apps, Emergency Numbers, and Local Contacts

Your phone can be your best companion in London — if you have the right tools. Technology helps you explore safely, connect easily, and find those hidden corners faster.

Here are a few must-have apps for urban explorers:

- **Citymapper:** For navigating public transport efficiently.
- **Google Maps (Offline Mode):** Perfect for when Wi-Fi drops out in tunnels or side streets.
- **Hidden London App:** Reveals secret sites and historical trivia.
- **Time Out London:** Helps you find local events, pop-ups, and community gatherings.
- **Uber/Bolt:** For safe rides anytime.

Always save important emergency numbers:

- **Emergency (Police, Fire, Ambulance): 999**
- **Non-Emergency Police: 101**
- **NHS Medical Help Line: 111**

Keep a note of your country's embassy or consulate in case of passport or travel issues. If you're renting an apartment or Airbnb, ask for local contacts — a neighbor, the landlord, or building manager. These small steps ensure peace of mind while you explore freely.

5. Mistake to Avoid: Ignoring Local Advice

If there's one mistake many travelers make, it's thinking they know the city better than the locals. Londoners may seem reserved, but they know shortcuts, favorite parks, and the best times to visit places you'd never find online.

Always take time to ask — whether it's your café barista, a taxi driver, or a museum volunteer. Locals appreciate curiosity when it's genuine. They'll often share stories or directions that lead you to unforgettable spots — like a hidden courtyard garden or a Sunday-only bakery.

Ignoring local advice can cost you experiences, not just convenience.
You might miss out on a quiet viewpoint, a special event, or even a safety tip that matters.

A great traveler listens, observes, and adapts. The best part? Locals remember kindness — sometimes leading to friendships that last long after your trip ends.

Traveling Smart, Staying Curious

Exploring hidden corners of London is about walking differently — with eyes open and heart ready. Safety, budgeting, and respect for local culture aren't just travel strategies; they're how you earn the city's trust.

When you plan wisely, stay alert, laugh with locals, and follow your instincts, London stops being a place on a map — it becomes a living, breathing story you're part of.

So, take these lessons as your urban toolkit. The more carefully you prepare, the more freely you can wander. And remember: the greatest discoveries often begin where the map ends.

Chapter 11

Meeting the Real Londoners

Have you ever wondered what truly makes London come alive beyond its famous landmarks and historic sites? It's not the buildings or the buses—it's the people. The real heartbeat of London lies in its locals: the shopkeepers who've worked the same stall for decades, the artists who transform forgotten corners into creative spaces, and the everyday Londoners who welcome you into their world with a story, a smile, or a pint.

In this chapter, you'll learn how to meet these locals, start genuine conversations, and experience the city through their eyes. Whether you're chatting in a cozy pub, joining a neighborhood clean-up, or taking a pottery class in Peckham, you'll discover that London's soul is best found through its people.

1. How to Strike Up Conversation in Local Pubs and Markets

Let's face it—many travelers love the idea of connecting with locals but feel unsure how to start. Londoners might seem reserved at first, but underneath that polite exterior, they're friendly, funny, and love a good chat—especially over a drink or while browsing market stalls.

The key is to start small and stay curious. In a pub, begin with something simple:

"Is this your local?" or "What's your favorite drink here?"

These open-ended questions invite conversation naturally. Pubs like **The Churchill Arms in Kensington** or The Southampton Arms in Kentish Town are perfect places to mingle because they attract regulars who enjoy conversation.

At markets—like **Borough Market**, **Broadway Market**, or **Maltby Street Market**—talk to the stall owners. Ask about the ingredients, the story behind a product, or what locals usually buy. You'll often find yourself hearing personal stories about family recipes or hidden food spots nearby.

Quick Tip: Londoners appreciate good manners. Always start with a smile, listen more than you talk, and don't interrupt. If you show genuine interest, they'll open up faster than you expect.

2. Volunteering and Community Events for Visitors

One of the best ways to meet real Londoners is through **volunteering**. You don't have to commit to weeks of work—many organizations welcome visitors for a few hours or a day. It's a powerful way to give back while learning about local life from the inside.

Charities like **The Felix Project** or **FoodCycle** let volunteers help prepare and distribute meals to communities in need. You'll meet locals who care deeply about their neighborhoods and hear stories that reveal a side of London not found in travel guides.

If you're interested in the environment, **Thames21** organizes river clean-ups, and **London National Park City** hosts green-space projects where you can plant trees or restore wildflower gardens. These activities are not only fulfilling but also create opportunities for meaningful connections.

Community events—like **street fairs, open-air film nights, or local festivals**—are another fantastic way to connect. Areas like **Hackney**, **Brixton**, and **Camden** often host cultural gatherings that blend art, food, and music. Attend with an open mind and you'll leave with friends, not just photos.

Action Step: Check out the website *Time Out London* or *Do-It.org* before your visit. Both list up-to-date volunteering and local event opportunities for travelers.

3. Creative Workshops and Neighborhood Classes

What better way to meet locals than by learning alongside them? London is full of creative workshops where you can paint, cook, craft, or dance with residents instead of tourists.

Try a **pottery class in Peckham**, a **photography walk in Shoreditch**, or a **bread-making session in Hackney**. Studios like **Turning Earth** or **Obby London** offer single-session workshops that welcome beginners. These small settings make it easy to talk, share laughs, and connect over a shared activity.

In **Brixton**, you might join a Caribbean cooking class taught by locals who have lived there for generations. In **Camden**, you could learn screen printing from artists who helped shape London's punk scene. Each class tells part of London's story—and lets you become part of it.

Personal Insight: When I took a calligraphy class in Islington, I ended up chatting with two Londoners who invited me to their favorite tea spot afterward. That spontaneous afternoon felt more "London" than any guidebook experience I've ever had.

Tip: Don't worry about perfection. Locals appreciate enthusiasm more than skill. Come curious, participate fully, and enjoy the shared energy of creating something new together.

4. Local Secret: The Londoners Who Know the City's Soul

Every city has its storytellers—the people who seem to carry its spirit wherever they go. In London, they're everywhere if you know where to look.

You'll find them running small bookshops in **Marylebone**, guiding street art tours in **East London**, or performing live music in hidden pubs across **Soho**. Some are taxi drivers who've memorized the city's 25,000 streets for "The Knowledge." Others are neighborhood historians who can point out which building was once a Victorian bakery or a 17th-century tavern.

One such gem is **Dennis Severs' House in Spitalfields**, maintained by locals who love to tell the stories of everyday life in old London. Another is **Daunt Books**, where staff often recommend not just books but personal favorite walks through literary London.

If you want to meet these storytellers, go where curiosity thrives: bookshops, independent cafés, historical societies, and local walking tours. Ask questions. Most of them love sharing insights with those who genuinely care about the city.

Local Secret: Visit the *Museum of the Home* in Hoxton. The volunteers there are passionate Londoners who can share how daily life in the city evolved over centuries. Their stories are like time machines in conversation form.

Meeting the real Londoners isn't about luck—it's about intention. You don't need a special invitation or fluent slang; you just need curiosity, kindness, and the courage to start a conversation. Whether it's a market vendor telling you where to find the best sausage roll, or a stranger at the pub recommending their favorite canal walk, these moments reveal London's beating heart.

When you leave, you won't just remember the places—you'll remember the people who made you feel at home in a city of millions. That's the real hidden corner of London: the one you find in someone's story.

Key Takeaways

- Start conversations in casual settings like pubs and markets—Londoners respond to curiosity and kindness.
- Volunteer or attend local events to connect meaningfully while giving back.

Above all, be genuine, respectful, and open. The city's real magic lives in its people.

CHAPTeR 12

CAPTURING THE HIDDEN SIDE

Have you ever wandered through London's quiet backstreets and wished you could capture the magic just as you felt it — without the crowds, noise, or distraction? This chapter is about doing exactly that. It's about documenting the hidden corners of London — not as a tourist, but as a storyteller. Whether through photos, journals, or thoughtful posts online, you'll learn how to preserve your discoveries while keeping their mystery alive.

1. Photographing the City Without Crowds

It's one of the biggest challenges in modern travel — how do you take meaningful photos in a city as busy as London without hundreds of strangers in the frame? The truth is, the best photographers aren't just lucky; they're patient observers.

Start by planning your timing. Early mornings, especially between 6 and 8 a.m., reveal a completely different London. The cobblestones of Covent Garden shine softly after rain, and even iconic spots like St. Paul's Cathedral can appear almost empty. Sunset hours also create golden tones that transform ordinary streets into cinematic scenes.

If waking early isn't your thing, explore lesser-known areas. Instead of Tower Bridge, capture the smaller bridges along the Thames Path. Rather than Oxford Street, wander through the vintage shop lanes of Marylebone or the pastel terraces of Primrose Hill.

Bring a simple, lightweight camera or even your phone — the goal isn't professional perfection but authenticity. Look for small details: an old sign, a door covered in ivy, a café window reflecting the skyline. These are the kinds of images that tell personal stories, not just tourist postcards.

Pro Tip:

Turn off your flash and shoot in natural light. Use quiet moments — early, cloudy mornings or just after rain — to capture a calm and moody atmosphere.

Action Step:

Pick one hidden corner near where you're staying — a mews, a canal path, or a quiet garden — and spend 15 minutes photographing only the details. You'll be surprised how much story hides in the small things.

2. Journaling Your Discoveries

A photograph freezes a moment, but a journal captures the feeling. Writing about your experiences gives your journey depth. It helps you remember not just what you saw, but how it made you feel.

You don't need to be a writer to keep a travel journal. Start simple. Each day, jot down where you went, who you met, what surprised you, and what you learned. Maybe it's the smell of roasted coffee in a small café in Clerkenwell or the sound of church bells echoing through an empty alley in Bloomsbury.

Use sensory details — what did you hear, see, smell, or taste? These details bring your memories to life later on. Journaling also encourages you to slow down and observe — something that's easy to forget in a city that never seems to stop moving.

If you prefer digital tools, apps like Evernote, Day One, or even Google Docs work well. The key is to write consistently, even a few lines a day.

Pro Tip:

End each journal entry with a reflection. Ask yourself: "What made today feel special?" or "What did I notice that others might miss?"

Action Step:

Carry a small notebook or use your phone's notes app. After visiting a hidden spot, write three sentences describing how it made you feel — not just what it looked like. Over time, these notes become your personal travel storybook.

3. Social Media Without Spoiling the Secrets

It's tempting to share every discovery instantly. After all, part of travel joy is showing others the beauty you've found. But in a world overflowing with travel influencers, there's a growing need to protect special places from overexposure.

When you find a quiet café in Hackney or a secret garden in Chelsea, think twice before geotagging. Sharing too precisely can lead to overcrowding and even damage delicate spots. Instead, focus your captions on emotions, lessons, or atmosphere — let mystery be part of the magic.

Share your perspective, not just your location. You could write, *"Found a small corner of London where time stands still,"* instead of *"Hidden café near Shoreditch High Street."* This keeps curiosity alive while preserving the authenticity of the place.

Pro Tip:

Create themed posts — "My Favorite Quiet Corners," "Moments of Stillness in London," or "Hidden Beauty in Everyday Streets." These engage readers emotionally while avoiding the "tourist map" effect.

Action Step:

Before posting, ask yourself: "Will sharing this help others appreciate London more — or will it take away its quiet charm?" Let that guide your choices.

4. Reflection: How Hidden Corners Change the Way You See London

When you slow down and explore hidden corners, you stop being just a visitor — you become part of the city's rhythm. You start to notice the small kindnesses, the sounds between the noise, and the life behind the scenes.

You might realize that London isn't just a capital of landmarks, but a collection of villages — each with its own heartbeat. From the laughter echoing in a Brixton market to the stillness of an early walk along Regent's Canal, you begin to see how the city breathes.

Reflecting on your journey helps you understand why these hidden corners matter. They remind you that beauty isn't always in grand monuments — sometimes, it's in the flicker of light through an old window or the quiet smile of a local vendor.

Pro Tip:

End your trip with a reflection day. Revisit your photos and journals. Ask: "Which moments meant the most?" You may find that your favorite memories aren't from the famous spots at all, but from the ones you stumbled upon by chance.

Action Step:

Write a short letter to yourself titled "What London Taught Me." Summarize your insights, emotions, and favorite discoveries. It's a simple but powerful way to close your journey and carry the lessons forward.

Capturing London's hidden side isn't about chasing perfection. It's about learning to see the unnoticed, to listen to silence, and to share responsibly. When you photograph thoughtfully, journal with emotion, and post with care, you create more than travel memories — you tell stories that last.

By the time you finish exploring, you'll realize that the real London isn't just on postcards. It's in the spaces between footsteps, the whispers of history, and the hidden corners waiting quietly for someone like you to notice them.

Key Takeaways

- Wake up early or wander late to capture quiet, crowd-free photos.
- Use journaling to deepen your emotional connection to each place.
- Share online responsibly to protect hidden gems.
- Reflect often — the best discoveries often change how you see the world.

CHAPTeR 13

Beyond Goodbye – Keep the Spirit of Discovery Alive

When a journey ends, something unexpected happens — part of you stays behind, and another part awakens. London has a way of leaving its mark on those who dare to explore its hidden corners. You've wandered down quiet mews, tasted coffee in tucked-away cafés, and found beauty where few tourists ever tread. Now comes the question every traveler faces: *How do you keep that sense of discovery alive once you're back home?*

This chapter is about turning your trip into something more lasting — not just a memory, but a mindset. Let's explore how you can carry London's hidden spirit with you, keep learning, and continue exploring, even when the suitcase is back in the closet.

1. Returning for More: Hidden Corners You Missed This Time

No matter how much time you spend in London, you'll never see it all. The city changes daily — cafés close, murals appear overnight, and secret gardens come alive in new ways each season. Many travelers make the mistake of thinking they've "done London" after one trip, but locals know the truth: the city is infinite.

If you found joy in discovering places away from the crowds, plan your next visit with intention. Instead of revisiting the same spots, create a "return list." Maybe it's that courtyard café in Bloomsbury you didn't get to, or the old bookshop in Hampstead you heard whispers about. Keep a small travel journal where you jot down discoveries and tips from locals. This becomes your personal "unfinished adventure" list — a promise to yourself that you'll come back, not to check boxes, but to keep connecting.

Actionable Tip:

Before you leave London, choose three neighborhoods you haven't explored yet and make a plan to return within two years. Treat each visit like a new chapter in an ongoing story rather than a repeat trip.

2. Similar European Cities with the Same Quiet Charm

London's hidden corners have a certain rhythm — a mix of history, culture, and understated charm. But it's not the only city that offers this. Across Europe, there are destinations where you can feel the same quiet thrill of discovery.

Lisbon, Portugal has narrow lanes, pastel buildings, and soulful Fado music drifting from neighborhood bars. **Edinburgh, Scotland** hides secret gardens and alleyways behind the Royal Mile. **Bruges, Belgium** offers cobbled streets and canal reflections that feel straight out of a storybook. **Ljubljana, Slovenia** mixes café culture with riverside calm. Each of these cities offers a slower pace — a place where you can get lost on purpose.

The key isn't to chase the same kind of trip. It's to carry the same *mindset* — to look beyond the obvious, listen for local stories, and notice small details most travelers miss. Once you've learned to travel that way, every place becomes full of hidden corners.

Actionable Tip:

Pick one European city that calls to you and explore it with the same curiosity you had in London. Research hidden alleys, family-run restaurants, and local hangouts — and let that guide your next adventure.

3. Staying in Touch with Locals and Fellow Travelers

The real treasure of any journey isn't always the destination — it's the people you meet along the way. Maybe it was a café owner in Notting Hill who told you where to find the best scones, or a fellow traveler you met while sketching by Regent's Canal. Staying connected to these people helps the experience live on long after the trip ends.

Social media makes this easier than ever, but go beyond just "following" people. Send a message, share your favorite photos, and thank them for the memories. Join local online communities or travel forums where people share lesser-known London finds. You'll not only keep the conversation going, but you'll also get insider updates about what's new or changing in the city.

Actionable Tip:

After each trip, write a short email or message to one or two locals you met. Express your gratitude, share a photo, and let them know their advice made a difference. This small gesture often leads to lifelong friendships — and even better travel tips for your next visit.

4. Sustainable Exploration: Respecting the Spaces You Find

Hidden places stay special only when travelers treat them with care. It's easy to forget that some of the secret gardens, quiet canals, or tiny shops you discovered are part of local lives, not tourist trails. The charm of London's hidden corners depends on the respect of those who visit them.

As a responsible traveler, aim to leave every place just as you found it — or better. Support small, family-run businesses. Use public transport or walk whenever you can. Avoid posting the exact location of hidden spots online if doing so might draw crowds or harm the environment. The goal isn't to *consume* the city but to *connect* with it.

You can also give back by volunteering, donating to local preservation projects, or simply choosing eco-friendly accommodations on your next visit. Every small choice contributes to keeping London — and other cities like it — authentic and alive.

Actionable Tip:

Adopt the "one good deed per trip" rule — whether it's buying from a local artisan, picking up litter in a park, or spreading awareness about responsible travel. It's a simple way to give more than you take.

The Journey Never Truly Ends

Leaving London doesn't mean the adventure stops. The real gift of exploring hidden corners is how it changes the way you see the world — and yourself. Once you've learned to find beauty in backstreets and meaning in quiet places, every city, every walk, even your own neighborhood, becomes richer.

Keep the spirit of discovery alive. Continue wandering with open eyes and a curious heart. Let every trip, big or small, remind you that the world is full of secrets waiting to be found — and that you now know how to uncover them.

Key Takeaway:

Travel is not about how far you go; it's about how deeply you see. The hidden corners of London have shown you that magic exists in the overlooked, and adventure begins the moment you look closer.

Conclusion

Congratulations on reaching the end of this incredible journey. You've walked through secret lanes, peeked behind historic facades, and wandered into corners that many travelers will never see. You've gone far beyond the postcard version of the city and found its hidden heartbeat. That's no small thing. It takes curiosity, courage, and a true traveler's soul to go where most people don't even think to look. So take a moment to celebrate yourself for exploring with open eyes and an open mind. You've not just read about a place—you've learned how to truly experience it.

From the very first page, this journey has been about more than sightseeing. It has been about discovery, about learning to see a great city from the inside out. You've learned that every narrow lane, every unmarked doorway, and every local café has a story to tell. You've seen that behind the noise and motion of the city lies a slower, richer rhythm that only reveals itself to those willing to pause and look closer. You've gone from being a visitor to being an explorer—and perhaps even a part of the story yourself.

When people travel, many rush to see the big landmarks. They check them off a list, snap a photo, and move on. But you've chosen something different. You've learned that travel is not about quantity—it's about connection. It's about looking up from the map and noticing the way the light hits an old brick wall, or how a local baker smiles when you ask about the recipe for their bread. It's about feeling the soul of a city that still lives in its hidden corners, waiting for someone like you to notice.

One of the most powerful things you've learned is to look beyond the obvious. You now know that the most meaningful discoveries often happen away from the crowds. You've learned to take detours, to follow that quiet alley that others ignore, to step into the small galleries, local bookshops, and forgotten gardens that hold a city's true charm. These moments remind you that beauty isn't always loud—it's often found in the gentle whisper of the ordinary. The joy of travel is not in being everywhere, but in truly being *somewhere*.

You've also learned that the people make the place. Talking with locals, sharing a laugh at a market stall, or sitting beside a stranger on a park bench teaches you more than any guidebook could. You now know that every city is made up of countless personal stories—and when you connect with the people who live them, you begin to understand the soul of the place. Locals don't just show you where to go; they show you how to feel. They open doors that lead not just into hidden spots, but into deeper understanding.

Another valuable lesson you've gained is the art of slow travel. You've seen that slowing down isn't missing out—it's what allows the magic to appear. When you walk instead of rush, when you sit quietly in a café and watch the world go by, you notice the life unfolding around you. You've realized that the real treasures of travel aren't always the ones on a map. They're in the laughter echoing down a backstreet, the smell of bread in the morning air, and the sense of being fully present in a moment that will never come again.

You've discovered that every neighborhood tells a story of its own. Each has its rhythm, its voice, and its secret places that reflect its spirit. You've walked through elegant lanes, creative quarters, and riverside corners, and you've learned that exploring these areas is like reading chapters in the same book. Each one adds a new layer to your understanding of the city and its people. When you take the time to wander through them, you discover that even in a city you thought you knew, there are endless surprises waiting around the corner.

Food has also been one of your greatest teachers. You've tasted flavors that carry history, love, and culture within them. You've found meals in tucked-away kitchens, tiny markets, and old pubs where recipes are passed down like family secrets. You now understand that food is not just nourishment—it's a language of connection. Every bite tells a story about the people who made it, the neighborhood it came from, and the traditions that shaped it. When you eat locally and thoughtfully, you're not just filling your stomach—you're filling your journey with meaning.

You've also grown into a more responsible traveler. You've learned that the way you explore matters. Being mindful of where you spend your money, respecting the communities you visit, and protecting the spaces you walk through are all part of the art of travel. Sustainable exploration means leaving places better than you found them, or at least ensuring they remain unspoiled for others to enjoy. It's about remembering that these hidden corners belong not just to us, but to future travelers and local generations yet to come.

Perhaps one of the most profound lessons you've learned is that exploration doesn't end when the trip does. The spirit of discovery is something you carry within you. Once you learn to see the world with curious eyes, you can find hidden corners everywhere—even in your own hometown. That same curiosity that led you down quiet streets can guide you through the patterns of everyday life. A familiar walk can become an adventure if you look closely enough. You've gained a way of seeing, not just a list of places.

You've learned to look beyond the obvious, to connect with locals, to slow down and observe, to understand the unique rhythm of neighborhoods, to savor authentic flavors, to travel responsibly, and to keep the spirit of exploration alive wherever you go. These are not just travel lessons—they are life lessons. They remind you to stay curious, open, and aware, not only when you travel, but always.

Now that you've reached this point, it's worth taking a moment to reflect on what kind of traveler you've become. You are no longer a tourist chasing attractions. You're a seeker of stories, a listener, a wanderer who appreciates the quiet beauty in the overlooked. You've learned that travel doesn't always need a grand plan. Sometimes it's enough to step outside, take a turn without a destination, and see what unfolds. You've learned to trust your instincts, follow your curiosity, and allow the journey to reveal itself.

But this journey doesn't have to end here. The city you explored will always have more secrets to uncover. Perhaps there were hidden corners you didn't have time to reach, small museums you meant to visit, or cafés you planned to return to. That's the beauty of travel—it always leaves something unfinished. It invites you back, whispering that there's more to see, more to feel, more to understand. Each visit will be different, shaped by the season, your mood, and the people you meet. And when you return, you won't just be revisiting a place—you'll be continuing a conversation you started long ago.

And when your curiosity takes you beyond this city, you'll find that many European towns share the same quiet charm. Places like Bruges, Ghent, Ljubljana, or Porto have their own narrow streets, local cafés, and layers of history hidden beneath their surfaces. The lessons you've learned here will guide you wherever you go. You now know how to see with attention, how to walk without haste, how to listen with heart. You'll be able to find the hidden corners not just in cities, but in people, in cultures, and in yourself.

You may also want to keep in touch with the people you met along the way—the local shop owners, the artists, the travelers who crossed your path. These connections are what keep the spirit of your journey alive. A message, a shared photo, or a return visit can strengthen those bonds. The relationships you build while traveling are threads that weave into the larger fabric of your life. They remind you that the world is vast but also wonderfully connected.

As you continue to explore, remember to travel with kindness and care. Be gentle with the spaces you visit. Take only memories and leave nothing but respect. The smallest gestures—smiling at a local vendor, picking up litter, choosing family-run businesses—can make a big difference. Traveling sustainably doesn't mean giving up adventure. It means ensuring that others can experience that same sense of wonder for years to come. The best travelers are not those who take the most, but those who give back quietly through appreciation and awareness.

Before you close this book, there's one simple way you can give back right now. If you enjoyed this journey, please take a moment to leave a positive review on Amazon. Your feedback helps others like you—people who crave authentic experiences—to discover this guide and use it to enrich their own travels. Reviews also help independent authors continue creating valuable books for readers who want more than the usual tourist path. It only takes a few minutes, but it makes a real difference. By sharing your thoughts, you become part of a circle of travelers helping each other find meaning and inspiration around the world.

You can also share this book with friends or family members who love hidden discoveries or are planning to visit soon. Perhaps they, too, are tired of crowded attractions and long for something more genuine. Your recommendation might be the spark that helps them experience travel in a whole new way. And who knows—you might even decide to explore together someday, trading notes about the corners each of you finds.

As you turn the final page, remember that this isn't really the end. The story continues every time you walk down a quiet street, sit by a river, or watch the city lights reflect on the water. The mindset you've gained—the ability to slow down, to notice, to connect—is a gift that will serve you for life. You've learned how to make any place feel alive, how to find the extraordinary in the ordinary. That's a rare skill, and it will change the way you see the world forever.

So keep going. Keep seeking out places that others overlook. Keep asking questions, trying new paths, and saying yes to the unexpected. The world is filled with wonders waiting just out of sight, and you now have the eyes to see them. Every journey you take from now on will carry the same spirit that brought you here—the spirit of discovery, of curiosity, of quiet awe.

Let this be your reminder that travel isn't just about moving through space—it's about expanding your awareness. It's about finding beauty in stillness, learning from people, and feeling grateful for the chance to explore. Each journey changes you a little, teaching you to live with more wonder, humility, and joy.

And as you step into your next adventure—whether it's across the sea or down your own street—take this thought with you: there are always new corners to find, even in the most familiar places. The world still has hidden stories to tell. All you need to do is look a little closer, listen a little longer, and walk a little further. Keep your curiosity alive, and it will lead you to magic again and again.

The adventure doesn't end when you close a book or unpack your bag. It lives on in your heart, in the way you notice details others miss, in the way you see beauty where before there was only routine. Wherever you go next, go with the same spirit that guided you here—gentle, open, and endlessly curious. Because somewhere out there, just waiting for you, another hidden corner is calling your name.

© **Selene draxwell**

Printed in Dunstable, United Kingdom